Desperate Times

Desperate Times

Pat Johnson

Writers Club Press

San Jose New York Lincoln Shanghai

Desperate Times

All Rights Reserved © 2001 by Patrick G. Johnson

Writer's Showcase
an imprint of iUniverse.com, Inc.

For information address:
iUniverse.com, Inc.
5220 S 16th, Ste. 200
Lincoln, NE 68512
www.iuniverse.com

ISBN: 0-595-17855-3

Printed in the United States of America

Dedicated to Mary Ross, my grandmother who encouraged me to read.

INTRODUCTION

On September 1, 1939, Adolph Hitler, the leader of Nazi Germany unleashed his military might against the hapless Poles. Using military tactics and weapons in ways never before seen in history, the German army and air force overwhelmed the Polish army in just 27 days. Britain and France declared war and fired diplomatic shots but for the next eight months, their guns were mostly silent. In the meantime Germany gobbled up Norway and intimidated Denmark into submission.

The British and French governments were in turmoil. Years of appeasement and arms reductions in hopes that Germany would follow had left them ill prepared for war. France now put all her hopes on their daunted Marginot defenses. Their combined forces were strong enough to have defeated Hitler had they moved east at the time of the declaration of war, but the losses and horrors of the last war left them paralyzed with fear. While Germany built her reserves and planned, the allies attempted to consolidate resources. The British sent the British Expeditionary Force, over 500,000 of the best British troops and what fighter aircraft that could be spared, to France.

On the 10th of May 1940, Hitler turned his forces against Belgium, Holland and France. They by-passed the French Marginot defenses and swept across France seemingly effortlessly in what became know as the blitzkrieg or 'lightning war'. The BEF fought gallantly in a long retreat across northern France. Finally, with their backs to the sea at Dunkirk and despite a failed rescue attempt by Britain, the British forces surrendered. Swinging south, the German army soon reached Paris. The French government, realizing the inevitable fled south to Marseilles. As the Germans entered Paris the government leaders boarded French naval vessels and went into exile in Algeria. The day after Hitler announced the fall of France and his complete domination of Western Europe, Paul Reynaud, the prime minister of France, despite leaving most of her military weapons back on the continent, announced to the world, France's intention of carrying on the fight from her possessions in North Africa.

The prime minister of England, Winston Churchill, soon found his country to be the lone nation in Europe opposing the German juggernaut. His one hope lay to across the vast Atlantic in the United States of America.

Churchill's optimism ignored the fact that the United States politically was not in favor of intervening in another European war. Churchill used a friendship with a pen pal he had begun writing to when he was Lord of the Admiralty, to beg for assistance. His pen pal, president of the United States, Franklin Roosevelt, sympathized, but was limited to what he could do to assist England. Roosevelt was nearing the end of his second term in office and was up against the tradition of only two terms for a president begun by Washington. Having guided the nation through the Great Depression of the 30's, Roosevelt had the support of the people, but the people had let it be known that war in Europe was not the business of the United States. Bills Roosevelt sent before congress requesting aid for Britain were continually shot down. Humanitarian aid had been approved, but convoys carrying the vital supplies to England were often turned back after sighting German U-boats that constantly patrolled the convoy routes. Slowly the American people and thus the congress saw the need in building up the military both in terms of manpower and weapons. Programs to assist American industry in producing military equipment and a limited draft were approved. Roosevelt's insistence that giving aid to England in terms of weapons and equipment would help prevent the United States from having to enter the war was met with cries of "America First!" from congress.

Roosevelt having decided he would have to seek another term in order to lead his country through another crisis, became less insistent and decided to bide his time, assured that events would soon force the country's hand.

As Churchill campaigned vigorously for American assistance, the Germans began an all out air assault on the British Isles. German air squadrons pounded British airfields and radar installations daily. The small but modern German surface navy patrolled the English Channel, swarming in retaliation whenever the British fleet ventured out to attack. The u-boat campaign in the Atlantic all but isolated England from her commonwealth nations and left her slowly starving to death. Raw materials were scarce and naval and air skirmishes with the Germans had to be well planned and executed in order to curtail losses to irreplaceable equipment.

Thus in October of 1940, the British Empire was in grave peril of collapse.

CHAPTER 1

Harry's mind spun with a whirlwind of thoughts as he lay on his bed in the small apartment assigned to him at the British Embassy in Washington, D.C. It was a little past six in the evening on Friday, October 11, 1940. Harry had just finished an exhausting day. The ambassador, Lord Lothian had run a marathon of meetings and briefings. Panic had begun. Things were not going well in the war with Germany and it appeared as if the Churchill government might fall. Lothian had stated that the British Parliament had called for a vote of confidence, set for tomorrow.

Lothian hadn't ventured to guess what the outcome might be but he indicated that, if Churchill fell, a new government would seek terms with the Germans. What this meant for the British delegation here in America, Lothian could only speculate. If the Americans stayed out of the war, Lothian did not anticipate a closing of the embassy. However, if the Americans decided to go to war, the Embassy would surely be closed.

In a smaller top-secret meeting with the ambassador, attended by Harry and two attaches, Harry learned that plans were being developed to possibly move a government in exile to one of the commonwealth nations. The Ambassador emphasized that this was only being considered; it did not mean the British government would abandon the United Kingdom to the Germans.

Through his official position and his contacts in the American government, Harry was quite aware of the dire predicament the British
Empire was facing. Since May, the Germans had isolated England and
continued to pound her cities and military installations with daily raids.
The loss of her best men and equipment at Dunkirk had left Britain
with little in which to defend against a cross channel invasion by the
Germans. Sixty-seven warships had been destroyed along with countless other ships when Churchill had attempted to rescue the forces at
Dunkirk. German aircraft had decimated the fleet. All that remained of
the vaunted British navy was spread about the Empire and would need
several more weeks to reach England. The void left by the destruction of
the home fleet had allowed the Germans to set her small, deadly fleet of
modern warships in position to control the English Channel. Aircraft
from the captured airfields of France and Holland allowed the warships
to patrol virtually unmolested by the British warplanes that attacked
daily from British airfields.

After the fall of France in June, England had just 250 aircraft left to
help in the defense of her homeland. Churchill had decided to husband
his supply and only let small sorties of ten to fifteen airplanes harass the
German fleet. Superior tactics and brave piloting is all that prevented
these small sorties from being wiped from the skies. Little could be
done about the reports of barges and other small boats being sailed
from the Rhine and German ports to the ports of northern France.
Everyone knew it was only a matter of time before the Germans began
their cross-channel invasion.

Churchill had tried to bolster his countrymen with bold, optimistic
speeches, while at the same time trying to coax the United States into
sending any and all aid it could. That was one of the reasons Harry was
now assigned to the British embassy in Washington.

Harry had been born Harold Lloyd, son of an English Lord and
diplomat and an American mother. He had spent his youth in a succes-
sion of small private English schools and had attended Eton, Oxford

and Sandhurst, the British military academy. He had served as a Captain in the British Army in India, second in command of a regiment of Ghurkas. The Ghurkas had a reputation as strong methodical warriors. Harry mirrored their traits. He participated in all the physical training and became proficient in the Ghurka's tactics. "Cool and calculating, Captain Lloyd is one of our best trained fighting men" Harry's commander had written in his efficiency report.

Following in his father's footsteps and much to his superior's dismay, Harry resigned his commission in 1935 to join the Diplomatic Corps. Harry excelled in his new career. He had a natural ability to gain the respect of friend and foe. His performance reports described him as possessing a cool and logical mind, along with a determined will and tough constitution. His first assignment had been as a minor diplomat in Berlin where he witnessed first hand the good and the evil of Nazism. After the Germans had attacked Poland and Britain's subsequent declaration of war, Harry was re-assigned to the embassy in Washington.

He had heard rumors this posting to Washington was due to his mother's insistence. Harry's mother, Kathleen, was born to an affluent Irish-catholic family. Her father, Patrick O'Hara was a behind-the-scenes man in Boston politics. It was said no one ran for office or was elected without asking Paddy O'Hara's blessing first. Paddy had not taken kindly to his only daughter marrying an Englishman, even when Harry's father had relented and agreed to a catholic wedding. The wedding was the only occasion the Lloyds and the O'Haras had ever been in the same room together or on the same continent for that matter. That the couple had survived twenty-two years together was testimony to their devotion to each other.

Most of the time Harry and his mother had lived in London, but on occasions had followed his father on assignments abroad. Most of his childhood memories were of the house in London.

Harry's father had died suddenly in 1932 and his mother had moved back to Boston and her family.

Harry's re-assignment brought mother and son together for the first time in nine years. The notification of his father's death had not reached Harry until ten days after the fact and he had not been able to attend his father's funeral. By the time he had been able to reach his mother with a message, she had already buried her husband and began readying for the move back to America.

Harry's mother had thrived in her new environment. She had developed a circle of friends that included Mrs. Roosevelt and many important financial and political power brokers. She introduced Harry into this group and it was at one of his mother's many social events that he met Harry Hopkins.

Hopkins was an old friend and right hand man of the President. Harry liked him from the start. He had known Harry's father and spoke of him often. Harry had hardly known his father and enjoyed hearing of him from others. Harry's father had often been gone for months at a time, leaving Harry and his mother to live in their London home. Hearing of his father from friends and colleagues helped paint a picture of what sort of man his father had been.

Harry knew Churchill's pleas for aid were in vain. Although the Prime Minister and Franklin Delano Roosevelt, the President of the United States, had become pen pals and good friends even though the had never met, the President governed a country ill-prepared for war.

In 1940, The U.S. was still just crawling out from the depths of the Great Depression and the majority of leaders in congress were staunch isolationist. The county's industry had slowly recovered but was almost entirely dominated by domestic production. Automobiles, refrigerators and other household appliances could be made in abundance, but orders for tanks, planes, guns and ammunition were few and far between. The United States had fewer than 300,000 men in uniform. War games held in Louisiana in May had shown huge gaps in the strategy, tactics and equipment of the United States military and that of the Axis powers now dominating Europe. As hard as Roosevelt tried, congress and the military leaders would not let him have his way in what Roosevelt called his 'lend-lease' policies. They argued that until their own troops had the equipment and supplies to defend the nation, they would not allow what little equipment now available to be given away.

Harry had reported these and other facts to Lothian as part of his job as liaison with the U.S. war department, but he knew Churchill had a habit of ignoring information that differed from his own opinion.

As he lay on the bed, he wondered again if he could denounce his British citizenship and accept American citizenship. He could not just stand by and let the fascists gobble country after country. As an American, he was sure he could get back into uniform and get into the fight. He was sure Hopkins could make it possible, but the nagging feeling that he would be turning his back on his father, kept surfacing, adding to the turmoil.

A knock at the door broke into his half-awake state. He flipped himself off the bed and opened the door. A British Corporal handed Harry a note and retreated down the hall. Harry shook his head in wonderment at the rudeness of the soldier, closed the door and opened the note. It was from Lord Lothian. It said there was to be an important military briefing in the War Department's Chiefs of Staffs conference room this evening and he was to attend. It was an order, not a request.

#

. Harry surveyed the room. The best military minds the United States had to offer sat in the worn brown leather chairs surrounding the large oak conference table. The far wall, at one end of the long table to Harry's left, held a large world map and chalkboard. They were not unlike the same found in the several schools Harry had visited. The dingy gray walls were lined with displays of men and weapons of the different branches of service. Behind him on the wall were several clocks that displayed the time for different regions around the globe.

The gathering was anticipating the arrival of Secretary of War Stimson and Chief of Staff General George Marshall. The men who had joined Harry in the conference room were all familiar to Harry. They were the brain trust of the U.S. Military: Admiral Stark, Chief of Naval Operations, Admiral King, General Arnold, Chief of Air Staff, and several of their staff members. No one seemed to mind that a foreign official was attending the briefing. With the exception of Admiral King, whom Harry had never met, they all knew Harry played a special role in the British Diplomatic Corps.

After the defeat of France, Prime Minister Churchill realized the necessity of bringing the United States into the war. He and President Roosevelt had agreed that a military liaison should be established between the two countries. Field Marshall Brooke was sent to work with the American Chief of Staffs and General Jacob Devers was sent to England. Because of Harry's special contacts within the Washington hierarchy, he was assigned to assist Brooke.

Brooke was a professional soldier, both in appearance and manner. He was one of Britain's key strategists in the war with Germany and the fact that he was sent to the United States was an indication of the importance of getting the U.S. into the war. Brooke knew little about the American military community but he knew a lot about Harry and his background. He even knew about Harry's dabbling in intelligence work while in Berlin.

British intelligence had asked Harry to see if he could get any information on the current rumored split in German intelligence. Harry had demurred, arguing that he did not understand how he was supposed to do this. As a minor official he had no access to any important German contacts. The challenge had intrigued Harry though, and in the end, he had set about it the only way he knew how.

He stole the documents from under the German's noses on a visit to the Abwehr's (German Army Intelligence Service) headquarters. He had made the visit on the pretense of seeing Elka, one of the secretaries he had been dating on and off. Though not large in stature, (Harry was only five foot ten) his handsome good looks, assured bearing, impeccable dress and intense blue eyes often attracted female companionship wherever he had been posted. On the day he stole the documents, he had followed Elka around the building as she showed him off to the other women secretaries. Although she had said he must wait outside, he had followed her into the copying room while she made copies of some papers. It was here he found lying in a stack of papers to be copied, an organizational chart for the Abwehr and an accompanying letter explaining the role of the Abwehr and the SD (Himmler's SS intelligence gathering department). While pretending to be overcome by passion he had pulled Elka to him in a passionate kiss with one arm while stuffing the papers into his coat pocket with the other. Fortunately, Elka was very pretty and the security details had hardly noticed him when Elka walked him out shortly after. Feeling guilty, he had broken it off with Elka a week later.

The intelligence folks were quite impressed and tried hard to recruit him for more work but although he did a few more minor tasks for them, Harry's superior pointed out that a diplomatic career was incompatible with intelligence work.

As time went by, Brooke began to rely on Harry increasingly.

Brooke was convinced the intervention of the United States was vital to the survival of Britain. He did not object to passing on to the U.S. military hierarchy information concerning British war intentions or diplomatic strategies. Brooke could never bring himself to directly give the Americans information outside of the scope of his official duties; instead, he passed the information on through Harry. As a result, the American military and political leaders were well informed on what was taking place in Europe.

Brooke felt confined in the liaison role and chaffed at the bit to command troops in battle. He often sent Harry in his place to meetings and briefings. After six weeks, Churchill had recalled Brooke to take over command of the Middle East forces and Harry was assigned the liaison duty full time.

Harry and the others were alerted by voices in the outer office. General Marshall, his aide, Colonel Eisenhower, and Henry Stimson, Secretary of War, entered the room.

"Be seated, gentlemen. I have some updates to give you on the situation in Europe then Ike will brief you on what the White House expects. General Marshall will then field any questions you may have." Secretary Stimson said as he walked over, pulled out the brown leather chair at the far end of the conference table to Harry's right and sat down. Marshall sat on his right. Eisenhower moved to an empty chair at the opposite end of the table.

Stimson opened the manila folder he had carried in with him, set it on the table in front him, and glanced around the table at the faces full of anticipation. His eyes fell upon Harry and Harry saw a brief nod from the Secretary. Harry's face remained impassive.

"This afternoon, the President received a telegram from Prime Minister Churchill," Stimson began. "Churchill is concerned about Britain's ability to hold out. He is also concerned about his own ability to keep Britain in the war. His political situation is in danger of collapsing. Numerous and serious setbacks in the war has led to questioning of his handling of the war.

"Britain's lifeline, tenuous as it is, has been hemorrhaging for the past 3 weeks under the onslaught of the Nazi U-boat attacks. Over a million and a half tons of shipping from Canada and private U.S. organizations has been lost. The British people are in real danger of starvation.

"The Luftwaffe continues to attack the airfields and radar stations in the south of England. While they are still managing to take three for every one of her planes lost in the air battles, Britain 's air forces are dwindling. Moving her squadrons to airfields in the north has drastically reduced the ability to intercept raiding parties before they can do any damage. London is being bombed as an aside to the main raids on her communications and airfields, and has suffered considerable damage. Over 25,000 citizens have lost their lives to the incendiary bombs the Luftwaffe is now using on British cities. The people are afraid and are letting their feelings known to parliament and the King. Unless some miracle happens; Germany attacks us or Congress unilaterally declares war, there may not be much more we can do to help the British."

"George, Ike, and I have just finished a meeting with the President and some members of congress. There are definite feelings about this recent news and Ike will brief you on them. Ike?" Stimson concluded by looking to Colonel Eisenhower.

Eisenhower stood and walked over to the map on the wall behind him. Turning to the room, he glanced quickly at the notes he held and began.

"As you know, President Roosevelt has been trying to do all he can to assist Britain in their struggle. Up to now, Congress' staunch support of neutrality has prevented us from doing more than selling food and a few obsolete arms to the British. He would like to offer his friend Churchill, more material aid. The President feels it is only a matter of time before Hitler does something stupid and provokes us into declaring war. With Churchill's downfall imminent and the possibility of a new government suing for peace, the President feels we should begin to do a little more to aid Britain in hopes of strengthening Churchill's government."

A rumble of surprised voices rolled around the table as members digested what was being said.

Ike, astutely recognizing the reason for the sudden outburst, continued: "The President isn't advocating an unprovoked attack, at least not by us. Nor is he advocating committing troops without a declaration of war. What he and certain members of Congress discussed were helping the convoys get to England with the material the British so badly need. We have countless vessels in mothballs and we can lease, that is to say, put under our flag, what is left of the British transports." Eisenhower paused and pointed to the Mediterranean Sea on the map. "The French government in exile in Algeria has offered the French fleet to help the British in the Middle East."

As he swept his hand in an arc from the East Coast of the United States to the British Isles, he continued, "Our Navy would provide escort from ports in the Western Hemisphere to ports in Britain. The exiled Danish government has offered the ports and airfields of Iceland to us non-gratis."

Turning back to the table, Eisenhower continued, "Feelings in congress have been slowly turning away from strict neutrality as the war has progressed. Farmers have already started to complain about the lack of export trade. Upset constituents have a very powerful effect on politicians." Ike added with a tight smile. He knew his audience had a narrow view of congress' handling of the crisis in Europe so far.

"In short, what has been decided is to drop the neutrality façade and openly aid the allies. No ground troops will be committed, but our Navy and Air Forces will be put to use providing cover and escorts for convoys." Ike paused and glanced at Secretary Stimson who nodded. Ike turned to Admiral King.

"Specifically, Admiral King, you are to notify Nimitz to begin moving ships from the pacific fleet to the Atlantic."

King glanced at Stimson then nodded.

Turning to General Arnold, Eisenhower continued.

"General Arnold, you are to begin moving fighters and medium bombers to the bases in Iceland."

Arnold frowned and bent to write something in his notebook.

Eisenhower turned his gaze back to the other members around the table and continued. "Tomorrow morning the President will announce our new foreign aid policy. In addition, he is going to announce the extension of our territorial waters to 500 miles off shore and will set a demarcation point dividing the Atlantic between the Americas and Europe. This will effectively cut the range of the U-boats or force them into our waters where we have the right to defend ourselves. General Marshall?" Eisenhower concluded his briefing by looking to General Marshall.

Marshall stood and walked around the table to the map. Stabbing with his finger, he pointed out various locations in Europe and North Africa. "Hitler has taken France, or at least the French soil on the European continent. With the exception of the channel, outside of his U-boats, he does not have a large enough navy to effectively challenge either the British or French navies on all the ocean routes. His buddy Mussolini is still stinging from the thrashing the combined British and French forces gave him in Ethiopia. What's left of the Italian navy is in port and it doesn't look like it's going to come out and play. Except for aerial attacks and a few U-boats, the southern Mediterranean is fairly safe for the French and British transports and war vessels.

"Our forces need to bring that same relief to the Atlantic. The U-boat menace is what is going to determine the success of a buildup in England provided she stays in the war. If she falls we still can build up in Iceland and use our naval forces to harass and attack Nazi fortifications and airfields along the coast. We need to keep the German armies and aircraft assigned to the coastal regions of France busy in order to keep them from reinforcing elsewhere." Marshall turned to face the table.

"Although we will continue to consider a landing on the French coast, I must emphasize our current strategy is to use North Africa for a staging ground to launch an attack on Italy. Italy is currently Hitler's weak underbelly. The Italians have proven to be poorly trained and poorly led. It appears to be the best region to attempt gaining a foothold back on the continent."

Marshall paused and looked at the map, collecting his thoughts. Satisfied he had covered what he a meant to cover; he turned back to group. "To accomplish any of this requires a massive increase in mobilization of our forces and an equal increase in industrial output. This is going to take time. Unfortunately, time is only one of the problems

Britain faces. Harry could you brief us on the current situation there?" Marshall looked to Harry and returned to his seat.

Harry, surprised by the request, rose and replaced General Marshall at the head of the table.

"As stated earlier, the coalition government is being attacked from many different powerful positions within parliament. Churchill's will power is all that is keeping it from falling. There is strong support in government to sue for peace. That force may be strong enough to oust the current government as early as tomorrow."

Harry paused as his statement sank in to the men gathered around the table. Eyebrows rose and murmurs of surprise rumbled around the table.

"While the political situation is bad, the military situation is critical." Harry continued by turning to the map and pointing to Scandinavia.

"The military has suffered terrible defeats in France and Scandinavia." Moving his finger to the Middle East, Harry continued. "While we have held our own in Africa, it has been costly. Almost all of our artillery and tank forces are in Africa and these have been depleted to a dangerous level. Until more heavy weapons can be brought in from your factories, any new offensive by Germany may result in the loss of Egypt and Persia. From there, it is short jump to India." He turned back to attentive faces.

"The failed attempt in Norway and the failed evacuation attempt at Dunkirk decimated our naval forces. Only 60 destroyers and eight battleships are in fighting condition. Hitler's military had spent the between war years developing strategies and aircraft for ground support. They have used these effectively in naval warfare also. We, on the other hand, believed as you did, that strategic bombing would be the power of the air forces. While we concentrated on bomber forces, we neglected fighter support. Consequently, we cannot effectively attack German bases in France or Holland. All attempts so far have resulted in large losses of aircraft and very little damage to German forces. The German air domination has allowed her to destroy our radar installations and fighter intercept bases in southern England. We have been unable to prevent German bombers from attacking British targets at will."

Harry focused his attention on Stimson and Marshall.

"I do not believe the efforts of your government will be enough to save the present government. I believe it would be wiser for you to plan your strategies around not having England, as a base of operations or her forces as a supplement to your own. We have not been told under what conditions peace terms would be accepted. I cannot speak for the navy or the dominions of course, but I truly hope that the naval forces and colonies do not fall into German hands, but it is a possibility." Harry concluded and returned to his seat.

Marshall thanked Harry as he returned to the front of the room. Sweeping his hand over the map of Europe he said, "Hitler holds all the cards. He has taken Europe from France in the west to Estonia in the east. The Balkans is still neutral but could fall to Hitler anytime he takes a notion to grab it. The French have about 750,000 troops available in North Africa but no weapons. All their artillery and tanks were left behind when they evacuated to Algeria. Stalin is pissing in his pants and has sent envoys both to the United States and Germany. He'll take the best deal offered. Since it doesn't appear we have much to offer, we can be assured he will stay in Hitler's camp for a bit longer, however, from reports we have received through the British, I think the Germans may soon have a surprise for him."

Turning back to the table, Marshall concluded, "Gentlemen, we need to figure out how we are going to mobilize enough trained troops to occupy Iceland, and build up in Africa. Officially, as stated, we are not committing any troops to combat as yet, but rest assured that that time is not far off and we will be ready when the inevitable occurs. The President intends to fire up the industrial community to begin massive production of aircraft, artillery, troop weapons, ammunition, tanks and ships starting tomorrow. Any questions?" Marshall folded his hands in front of himself and raised his brow in anticipation of questions.

"I'm sure the President knows what he is doing, but if we strip the pacific, what about Japan?" Admiral King was the first to ask.

"The President feels he can keep Japan at bay by loosening our embargo. The first ships and sailors we turn out will be sent to Hawaii to fill the gaps. You will confer with Nimitz tomorrow morning, and give us the best estimate of what forces you need to retain in the Pacific while supporting our efforts in the Atlantic." Marshall answered.

An Army colonel was next. "We all saw what Hitler and his panzers can do. We also learned from Louisiana just how inadequate our forces are. We need to completely rebuild our tank corps and machines to compete with them."

Ike responded to this. "Hitler has very few tanks available to him in Tripoli. We can control his reinforcement there with the French and the Good Lord willing, British fleets. In the meantime, as fast as we turn 'em out, we can buildup our own mobile forces in Africa. A French Colonel, DeGaulle is somewhat of a student of tank warfare and he was one of the few commanders who did well against the Germans before the fall of France. He has offered to train our commanders and troops. General Patton has some ideas on training our armored divisions also."

"Of course, you are aware, general, that the draft Congress implemented has only been in effect a very short time." General Arnold said.

"That partial mobilization drive three months ago has allowed us to build up both the Navy and Army rosters. We should be able to field between 20 and 50 divisions in the next few months. The industrial buildup the President is planning will provide you and your troops with the most modern aircraft very soon."

Marshall saw Stimson glance at his watch. He raised his hands indicating he would take no more questions and finished with; "Now I want each of you to begin working up a mobilization plan for your respective services to be on my desk by 1600 tomorrow. The President plans to name a war council soon. They will handle the details, but I want something to start with."

Walking back to his seat, General Marshall concluded, " This will be a massive undertaking. But I am sure we can do it. Thousands of British citizens are dying each day; thousands of French civilians have disappeared from their homes. There are reports that ethnic groups are being rounded up in Poland, Italy, France and Germany and being sent to what the British call concentration camps. Hitler does not play well with others and it is time he learned. The American people will not let this black cloud hang over Europe much longer. Declared war or not, we must be ready to fight. Thank you gentlemen."

Stimson rose and spoke as he gathered his papers, "If you'll excuse me, I have other affairs to attend to. As do you."

As Stimson and the General began to walk out of the conference room, Marshall glanced at Harry and nodded that he should follow. Harry nodded in acknowledgement. He watched the others gather their notes and begin to file out of the room. Admiral King stared at Harry with a perplexed look but said nothing as he too, turned and walked out of the room.

Harry rose from his chair, walked over to the map and frowned. "You yanks are going to need to get your asses in gear if you intend to do anything about this mess." he thought. He turned and walked out into the hall.

CHAPTER 2

Winston Churchill had received his response from President Roosevelt late Saturday night. The President had offered as much as he could but it would not be in time. Now, at half past one Sunday morning, he paced up and down the floor of his upstairs office in Chartwell, his country home. Although, since his rise to Prime Minister, he no longer stayed at Chartwell full time, he often came here alone to think.

The day had not gone well in parliament. The coalition he had fought so hard to put together was slowly unraveling. Too many setbacks had been encountered in their struggle. Norway, France, loss of control of the channel and the U-boat threat had cost Britain dearly. Churchill himself had been surprised at the swiftness of the German army. Unlike the last war, armies now required fast heavy armaments to command the battlefield. Coupled with Germany's innovative use of air power, her mobile forces were unstoppable. At least this had proven true with the weapons Britain had deployed. Artillery, which had proven so effective in the fields of Flanders and Verdun in the last war, was now too slow to be effective. The effects of Chamberlain's appeasement policy were now coming back to haunt Churchill and his war cabinet. Not enough ships, tanks, aircraft or transports existed in their inventory to counter the losses inflicted by the German war machine.

Despite being out-numbered, the air defense forces had done well early on, thanks in no small part to the radar and radio stations along the coast. However, despite the tremendous losses suffered by them, the Luftwaffe continued to pound away at these relay stations as well as the southern air bases. The number of planes and skilled pilots began to slowly erode. Where they had first been able to send 15 or 20 planes up to meet the attackers, they could only now achieve half that. Compounding the problem, the remaining air defense had to fly from bases farther north and often missed the attackers altogether or caught them on their way out.

The lack of anti-aircraft batteries was telling in the devastation of the southern facilities. The war cabinet refused to move what meager guns they had from the defense of London to the bases and radar stations where they could have been more effective. His argument that the more aircraft that were destroyed near the coasts cut down the number that would make it to her cities, had met with staunch opposition.

He had known for some time now that his influence over the decisions of the war cabinet was slipping. In a democracy, there are no autocratic leaders and he could not force his will upon them. He had pinned his hopes on America entering the war with all her manpower and industrial might before it was too late. He devoted considerable time to cultivating his friendship with the President with this as his aim.

Franklin Roosevelt was true friend. At the risk of his own political career he had unwaveringly supported France and Britain during the early dark days of the war. In defiance of the American Congress, Roosevelt had attempted to open the stores of the great democracy's arsenal to allow Britain to come and get what she needed to fill her own inadequate war supplies. His offer had also applied to the French who had lost all with the overrunning of their native European soil. Congress had proven too stubborn though and very little in military hardware had been released.

His personal plight was desperate. Crowds no longer cheered him. The people had the air of defeat all around them. Where once signs of encouragement had greeted him, signs now called for the end to the bombings and rationing. The people were war weary.

The opposition had called for a vote of confidence. Parliament would meet Monday. He didn't know if he had enough votes to defeat them. Any new setback or well-delivered attack on him and the national coalition could be enough to send him on a permanent holiday. Churchill was a veteran politician and knew that the President's latest announcements would not be enough to stem the tide of opposition. He also knew that if his government fell, there were several members of the opposition that was set upon asking Germany for terms. He had no doubt that if he were to be dismissed, this would occur.

All the papers had printed the recent speech by Ribbontrop, the German foreign minister. The speech had been filled with the references to the comradeship the German people felt for her English friends; Of how Churchill and his warmongering government had forced Germany into bombing Churchill's war making capabilities (no mention of why it was necessary to fire bomb civilians.) Ribbontrop had said that if the British people had the good sense to toss Churchill and his dangerous cronies from office, Germany would offer the best of terms and allow the island nation to live in peace.

Had not the people learned that the word of Hitler was worth nothing? Had they forgotten Czechoslovakia or Poland? Hitler would never allow Britain to keep her colonies. The Empire was doomed. A Britain with a fleet, no matter how decimated, was a threat to German dominance. Hitler would seize the colonies. The British fleet would be absorbed into the German navy. The democracy the British people held dear would be trampled beneath Nazi hob-nailed boots. There had been rumors for some time that Edward would be returned and placed upon the throne if the Germans defeated the British. Would the people stand for that?

Few listened when he spoke of the Nazi menace in the years before they showed their true face. Few would listen now. A stop to the bombing, food for all and a return to normalcy were on the majority of the people's minds. They would get all but normalcy he feared.

He would telegraph his friend, Prime Minister King of Canada. Perhaps, if the Germans took England, he could convince the King to move the government to Canada or perhaps Australia to carry on the fight, following the French lead. The thought of splitting the government reviled him, but he could not allow the Empire to perish, not while the powerful U.S. still had the ability to change the situation for England. If the King balked, he would go it alone.

Another telegraph would go to the British Ambassador in the United States. There was still a lot he could offer his friend Roosevelt.

CHAPTER 3

Marshall was already seated at his desk when Harry entered the General's office. The office was not large. Covering one wall were wooden bookshelves, filled with books on making war, weaponry and surprisingly, politics. Photographs, military decorations and various awards hung on the wall behind the desk. There were two dark-red leather tall-backed chairs directly in front of the desk and a dark-red leather couch on the opposite wall. Secretary Stimson was not present. He was surprised to see Harry Hopkins seated on the couch.

"Harry!" Hopkins exclaimed as he rose from the couch, offering a hand, "Glad to see you made it."

"Mr. Hopkins. "Harry said formally, as he shook the elder man's hand. "I'm a bit surprised to see you here."

"Good to see you again, Harry. "Hopkins winked and pointed to the leather chairs. "Sit down and we'll get into why I am here." Hopkins moved to the chair next to Harry's.

"The President was concerned that the military may not be as enthusiastic as he is about his proposals." Hopkins began. "He sent me to assist George here in answering any questions that may arise."

"Okay. That explains why you're here, but why am I here?" Harry asked, looking first to Hopkins then to Marshall.

"Harry," Marshall replied," You're here because both the President and I agree that your unique position and training can be of service to both our countries. The President is very concerned about Churchill's ability to stay on as Prime Minister. If he loses a vote of confidence, he could damn well be tossed out. He is the only leader you have over there with the guts to stick it out until we can formally get into the war. If England folds it's cards and sues for peace with Hitler, all of Western Europe is lost, not to mention your colonies. Hitler won't waste any time after that in going after Russia. He hates communists almost as much as he hates Jews. His fear of a two front war is all that has stopped him from tearing into Russia so far. France is no threat to him because they lack the resources to get back onto the continent. Hitler could care less if France rules all of Africa as long as she stays out of his new back yard. Besides, his Afrika Corps in Libya has been able to keep the British at bay in Egypt and Persia on one side and the French in Algeria and Tunisia on the other side. If England falls, he can turn the full power of his forces on French North Africa. Without our industrial might and manpower neither France nor England can put up any kind of fight that would threaten Hitler's dominance of Europe."

"I'm sorry General, I know all that, but I still don't see how you need me." Harry interrupted.

Hopkins turned to face Harry as he said: " We have very good reason to believe that you folks have improved on the Polish decoding techniques of the German Enigma ciphering machine. The intelligence derived from this is of the highest priority. It could greatly assist in countering Hitler's moves. Unfortunately, under your current situation, you cannot take advantage of it. If Churchill is ousted, we need you to get that intelligence before the Germans realize you have it and take it from you."

"What the hell is an Enigma machine?" a confused Harry asked. "I've never heard of it. Besides, if its secrecy is that well maintained, how did you find out about it?"

Hopkins leaned forward and clasped his hands over his knee, as he crossed his legs. Speaking directly to Harry, he replied: "The Enigma machine itself is not a secret. We've known about it for over ten years. In fact, we had the foresight to purchase a commercial Enigma in 1928 before it was withdrawn from the market. Unfortunately, we have spent more time using it in an attempt to decipher Japanese signals, but little concerning the Germans. The machine we have is outdated and I am told, barely resembles the military version now in use by the Axis.

"The Germans believe it to be invincible and are quite arrogant about it. They actually demonstrated their Enigma to Major Evans of our Army Signal Corps back in '29. They showed him versions of a large 10-rotor machine and an even larger 20-rotor machine. But we believe even the Germans have found them to be difficult to use and have stuck with the three rotor standard.

"Mr. Churchill has kept us informed on your progress in decrypting messages sent with the Enigma, although not the techniques. From time to time he has even released decrypted messages to us when it concerned U.S. interests."

Harry was astonished by this news. It wasn't that he didn't believe Hopkins, he was just was amazed that with such a weapon, his government had had such setbacks in the war.

"And you want me to find this machine, steal it and bring it back to your boys." Harry asked skeptically and added. "Since I have never heard of it, I doubt very much I can get access to it. A lowly official like me isn't likely to be given that kind of confidence."

"That's why we need your skills and training, Harry." Marshall interjected. "If anyone can get in and out with a prize like this, you can. You still have your British passport; you are still a Royal Subject. Getting you in won't be any trouble at all. Churchill has instructed Eden to assist you. Since Eden has been retained as the foreign minister, his assistance should open some doors for you. As far as getting you out again, we have devised a plan using the new Iceland bases to get a flight in to pick you and your package up."

Harry frowned. He felt his anger growing. His American 'friends' were calmly asking him to actually conduct treason against his country.

"You realize if the Churchill government does fall, what you are asking me to do is treason." Harry said as he rose from his chair and began to pace the floor behind Hopkins.

"What if I told you that Churchill has sent a message to your boss, Ambassador Lothian, stating that, in the event of a capitulation on Britain's part, your embassy is to turn over any and all intelligence the United States deems necessary?" Hopkins asked. He did not turn to look at the pacing Harry behind him but stared directly at Marshall.

"If such a message existed, I'm sure I would be aware of it." Harry replied. "The ambassador doesn't keep secrets from me. After all I am his conduit to you folks for all of his 'unofficial' contacts."

"Oh the message exists all right. Mr. Churchill wired the President about it a short time ago." Hopkins said turning towards Harry. " And before you begin arguing that it's intention is only for intelligence here in the U.S., we prefer to interpret it differently."

Harry thought this over. If the message existed, and it may very well exist, then any action taken on the American's behalf could be pardonable. Harry had pondered during the day how he could continue to fight if the unthinkable did happen. He knew he had no chance of getting his commission back and fighting as a soldier for one of the dominions. The foreign office saw his American ties as too important. He would probably be ordered back to England. On the other hand, he could seek asylum here and stay with his mother. No, that wasn't a real choice. There was but one choice.

"You get me a copy of the message." Harry looked directly at Hopkins "Better yet have Churchill wire me directly authorizing what you say the message authorizes, and I'll play ball, as you American's say."

"That a boy Harry. You saved me from having to deliver my 'for God and Country' speech. There is no one here or in your own government that doubts your loyalty. You can be sure of that. You'll get your message."

CHAPTER 4

The debate was proceeding just as Churchill had foreseen. After nearly seven hours of arguments, during which Churchill had not spoken, he felt it was time to end it. He rose and stepped to the podium. With the exception of a few subdued calls for Churchill to explain himself and the action of his cabinet, the entire assembly grew quiet

"Twelve months ago, Mr. Chamberlain stepped down and submitted my name to the King as his replacement." Churchill began, "I told you then I have nothing to offer but blood, toil, tears and sweat. I accepted the challenge and under your overwhelming acceptance, set about on the task of seating a cabinet that was diverse and strong. This coalition government consists of members of all parties represented here today. Our joint task was of defending the Empire from Nazi aggression and righting the direction in which previous governments, however well intentioned, had wrongly steered us. We have seen in France, in Norway, in Africa, and here in our gallant struggle with the German Air Forces, how woefully prepared we were and are for war. I do not tell you this in defense of actions, rather as the facts. Truth is incontrovertible. Panic may resent it; ignorance may deride it; malice may distort it; but there it is.

"Our present situation, as discouraging as it may seem, does not foretell the future. We have the will and are now building our resources to defend this Empire, and I daresay, to defeat the Nazi menace. The politician's job is to do all in his power to prevent war and protect the people's property and safety. When political means fail and war is thrust upon us, it is time for the politician to step aside and allow the warrior to do his job. Let us allow our warriors to do their job. Let us do all in our means to give him the tools to do his job. Let us not again seek to appease the enemy but join hands with other nations allied against tyranny and subjugation! Remember that an appeaser is one who feeds a crocodile, hoping it will eat him last. That crocodile is now looking for his last meal; we will not nurture him further. Let us continue to fight for what is right, what is just and most of all, fight for our very existence!

"Many of you have quoted the speech by Herr Ribbontrop. You have failed once again to see the enemy as he really is. We tried in the past to negotiate with the Nazi government. We received assurances that all we agreed upon would be adhered to by both parties. We are all aware of Hitler's history of broken promises: Versailles Treaty provisions, Locarno pact, Anglo-German Naval Agreement, demilitarized Rhineland, guarantee of Czech borders after Munich. The Czech borders his "last territorial claim in Europe". But I ask you, where now is Poland? Where now is Czechoslovakia? Belgium, Luxembourg, Lithuania? Latvia? Estonia? The list of countries that have bowed to or have been overrun by the tyrant Hitler is long. I do not intend for us to be added to that list!

"Are we to perish without a fight? Are we to once again bow to the demands of despot? What do you believe will be the result of an armistice with Hitler? Will the Empire remain? Will our proud navy relinquish the seas without a fight? What of India, Burma, Persia and Egypt? Will they remain with us? Will Hitler allow them to remain with us? And Canada, South Africa, and Australia? Only fools believe we will be allowed to rule our Empire after dealing with the Nazis. Believe me when I say, Hitler will rule our Empire! We may be lucky to rule our back yards!

"What of our people? We know thousands of French citizens are carted away to the inner bowels of the Third Reich everyday. The same is occurring in each of the countries the Nazis now control. Will we allow our citizens to become slaves of the Germans? Peace with the Germans will be all but peaceful! I never claimed England could defeat the powers of Germany and Italy alone. We need only to survive until other free democracies rise against the Axis tyranny. Even now, as we debate the future of our beloved Empire, America is awakening to lend her mighty power in our struggle. If we abandon our course, if we bow to the Axis now, we shall ever more be lost. The Empire shall fall! I daresay the sun shall finally set on the British Empire.

"The Nazis have used terror to weaken our resolve. They have attacked our cities and civilians alike. But we still stand! We still fight! We cannot at this hour desert our posts!

"It is now time for you to decide. Shall we relinquish the British Empire to the hands of the Nazis or shall we continue to fight tyranny and fight for our own existence? I warn you now. I have not become the King's First Minister in order to preside over the liquidation of the British Empire. I will continue to struggle against the fascist tyranny however and wherever I can. I have faith in our allies and I have received confirmation that the United States will soon be lending all her weight to our cause.

"I will remain steadfast to our democratic ideals, I will continue to believe in our peoples and our sovereign. Cast aside this grand coalition and cast aside the British Empire if you dare, for no matter your decision, I shall continue to be her champion. I say you have only to endure to conquer. You have only to persevere to save yourselves. "

Churchill concluded his speech amongst splattered applause and jeering. He did not know how the assembly would vote but no matter the outcome, his decision had been made.

The Prime Minister did not wish to stay for the rest of the debate and followed by catcalls and shouts, he left the chambers for Chartwell.

#

Chartwell had always been his bastion of hope. Here he could always find the tranquility he so much needed. However today, even Chartwell failed to give him much solace. As he climbed the stairs headed for his study, Churchill felt the weight of the Empire on his shoulders. In his heart, Churchill knew he had lost. Fear had gripped Parliament today and fear would rule their decision.

Settling into his favorite chair, with a brandy in hand, Churchill mulled over his options. Last night he had wired William Mackenzie King, Prime Minister of Canada. King had assured him his government would not follow with a petition for peace if England herself chose that route. Churchill, friends and family would be welcome if he so desired. Although they had had their differences over the use of Commonwealth soldiers, he had received the same response from Menzies in Australia. The avenues existed for him to carry the fight. The thought of dividing the Empire by choosing to ignore any government seated in England and carrying the fight from one of the Commonwealth nations or the Dominions, hung heavy on Churchill's heart. It was against all he had been taught and believed. However, the mere suggestion that Britain should bow to the Nazi evil sickened him more. Accepting a place in one of the Commonwealth nations would probably restrict his ability to directly influence the conduct of the war, something he believed himself to be immensely suited for, but he would be free to help. He understood his enemy now and could reasonably predict his actions and motives. How had the people and her elected officials been so fooled? Was human nature so thoroughly in need of comfort that it was willing to loose all? Did they not see the evil of the enemy?

He finished his drink, rose and walked to the cabinet that served as a bar. He would enjoy another afternoon aperitif and perhaps a nap while he awaited the outcome.

Two hours later, his butler, Inch, awakened Churchill.

"Sir, Mr. Eden has arrived and wishes to speak with you. He says it is urgent."

"Please, send him in. I dread the news but time will not lessen it." Churchill said as he rose from the bed. "I'll meet him in the study."

Anthony Eden, Churchill's foreign minister and good friend, entered the study and stopped to take in the sight of his friend before him. Churchill's hair was unkempt and Eden could tell he had just awoken. Churchill's ability to sleep anywhere and during any crises was legendary.

"Winston, the chamber has finished its debate just under an hour ago. The results are not good. The opposition carried the vote. We managed but 125 in our favor."

"I suspected as much. Have they asked for my immediate dismissal?"

"They have. They wish you to recommend Attlee as First Minister to the King."

"Then I shall. Straightaway. Please make yourself a drink. I have a fresh supply of Hind if you wish. I will go and make myself presentable and telephone the King that I am on my way. I do not wish to serve those that do not want me any longer than is necessary. Could you please telegraph Mr. Roosevelt and tell him of the outcome? I will write him in time with my own thoughts but it is imperative he know the situation here as soon as possible." With this Churchill left the room and crossed the hall to his bedroom. Eden walked to the telephone.

The King was aware of the vote and would see Churchill as soon as he could get to Buckingham Palace. As the car sped through the streets, Churchill surveyed the devastation the German bombing had caused. Houses were gutted and piles of debris littered the street, forcing his driver to zigzag through the streets. Churchill became more morose. What would become of England now? Attlee would surely ask for terms from Hitler. The people had spoken; they no longer desired to suffer the devastation and deprivations of war. Would the King share their feelings? If he could rally the King to his side, perhaps together they could carry the fight forward, if not from England then from abroad.

Churchill was led into the King's office. King George, contrary to tradition, stood, and walked to meet him extending his hand. Although he had a smile on his face, his eyes betrayed his weariness and sorrow.

"Your Majesty." Churchill said, bowing slightly before taking the proffered hand. "I am sure you are informed of the decision of your Parliament?"

"I'm truly sorry Winston. I do not agree with the decision but feel compelled to abide by it. Of course I could refuse to accept your resignation but we both know that would accomplish little but intensify the confusion."

"Yes. I have considered refusing to resign but I do not think it would be in your Empire's best interest. Therefore, please accept my resignation effective immediately. I recommend you call Mr. Attlee and ask him to form your new government."

"As we are old friends, Winston, I will tell you that he has been summoned already. I will suggest to him that the new government continue the struggle but you and I both know that is unlikely. I believe Hitler's plan for invasion is a bluff, that we need only to hold on for a few more weeks, and we shall have the Americans on our side.

"I too believe it is but a short time before the United States enters the fray with all the might of their men and materials, but I do not think Mr. Attlee is so optimistic. He and Ambassador Kennedy have had many discussions on why America should not become involved. Mr. Kennedy's ideas are, thankfully, in the minority now. The President has taken large steps toward entering this war already. If we capitulate, I believe he would still go forward but his options will be limited."

"I do hope he shall bring his mighty nation into this struggle but I believe it will be too late for us."

"What will you do, sir? I do not think Hitler will look kindly on you seated on the throne after all you have said condemning him. I should think you might consider going to one of the commonwealth nations or the dominions."

The King smiled.

"I believe that is why we have worked so well together, Winston." He paused and motioned for Churchill to sit in one of the high-backed chairs that stood before his desk. As he walked around his desk he continued, "The royal family will be leaving in the morning on the Royal yacht for a visit of the commonwealth. It may seem as if they are abandoning ship to our subjects, but I believe lives may be at stake here and I will not risk my family."

Churchill remained standing. The King hesitated for a moment then decided to be seated. Winston noticed the tired motions of man who carried a great burden.

"I understand perfectly sir. It is best you and your family get out of harms way as soon as possible. Hitler is not to be trusted. I myself, intend to take my family to Canada."

"I will not be going. At least not until the fate of the Empire is known." The King explained, then lowering his eyes and staring at his folded hands, he said: "Winston, unfortunately, your speech today has made parliament anxious. I have been asked to revoke your travel papers until the decision of negotiations with the Germans is complete. I am afraid they believe you would attempt to form your own government from abroad. You would not ascertain such an endeavor would you?"

Churchill raised his eyebrows and his pug face reddened. He could not believe what he was hearing.

"Surely, this recommendation is not one you need accept! Are you saying sir, that you forbid me from traveling under my own free will?"

Inwardly, Churchill was seething. He and the King had taken to having lunch together each Tuesday and he believed they had developed a solid friendship as well as an understanding.

"Your family is under no restrictions whatsoever. They may leave at any time. Winston, you of all people can understand what an action of that sort would do. It would pull the Empire apart. We would have Englishman against Englishman. I cannot have that happen. I will acquiesce to their request for now. But I assure you, once the negotiations are completed, your papers will be returned to you and you will be free to travel about as you wish."

No longer able to contain his anger and forgetting his place, Churchill moved to the front of the desk and leaned forward with both hands supporting on the desktop.

"With all due respect sir, Hitler has not even set foot on our shores yet and we have begun using his methods! I protest such treatment! It is grievous that such action is taken against a former member of your court!"

King George sighed and raised his head to look at Churchill. His eyes with a pleading look.

"Winston, you have served me and your country well. Your loyalty to the crown and to the Empire is not in question. I ask you to please stick with me during these dark times. Do as I ask. I will make it up to you if it is within my power. If the roles were reversed, I believe you would understand my position."

Churchill eyed the King with as near contempt as he could muster for his friend and sovereign. He knew further protests were useless. He would retire now from the argument while his temper was still in check. He had to think his options through, and here with the King, that would be impossible.

"Your Highness, you have my resignation and my recommendation. I know you are a very busy man now in such times, so I will bid you farewell." Turning to leave, Winston proclaimed " God save the King!" Again ignoring protocol, he walked from the King's chambers.

The King said no more and watched his former Prime Minister leave. He was overwhelmed with sadness. The old and tried British democracy had served her well through the centuries and he was sure she would again. But guilt and nagging doubts still filled his mind. "God save the King, indeed." He said to himself.

Churchill sat in the back of the car while the driver wove his way to Chartwell. Clemmie and the girls would be there by now. It was imperative they leave England at once and he would ensure they were out on the next ship sailing for Canada. He would be busy himself covertly trying to drum up support for furthering the war effort from somewhere within the Empire. He preferred Canada where he could be near his friend and ally, President Roosevelt. He had no illusions. If he stayed, he faced mortal danger.

CHAPTER 5

"I knew it! I knew we could break the British will!" Hitler exclaimed as he strode the floor of his office triumphantly before Ribbentrop.

"Churchill resigned without a fight you say? Excellent! Soon I will meet this man. In his cell!" Hitler cackled obviously enjoying his latest political victory.

"Yes, mein Fuehrer. Churchill stood before the King within two hours of the vote. Attlee was summoned by the King and is now Prime Minister. He has cabled us wishing for a meeting."

"Tell him to come as soon as he can." Hitler ordered then stopped pacing and turned to Ribbontrop.

"No. Tell him to be here tomorrow. We will give him our demands before he has time to think things over."

#

Clement Attlee received the German reply to his cable somberly. He chose Anthony Eden and Lord Halifax to accompany him to Germany; the former because he was his choice for foreign secretary and the latter because of his past experience as foreign secretary. Parliament and the war council had given him carte blanche to negotiate an end to the hostilities. He knew their faith was bolstered by the words of Herr Ribbontrop. Now as he flew across the channel with Halifax and Eden, he pondered the wisdom of such faith. Churchill had cried foul every time the Chamberlain government had dealt with the Germans and in the end he had been proven right. Again Churchill had warned against dealing with the Germans, but Attlee prayed he was wrong this time. Churchill reveled in his role as war leader and perhaps this clouded his judgment. Surely Churchill knew the country could not stand the U-boat blockade and bombings any longer. The people had lost the will to carry on the struggle. They had called for Attlee's leadership and it was he who would deliver them from their suffering.

Totally ignoring the lessons from Chamberlain's naiveté, Attlee firmly believed Hitler could keep his promises if you negotiated with good faith. Attlee believed himself to be realist enough to know that some demands placed upon them were going to be painful, the Empire would be divided he knew, but what was the alternative? Further destruction of England's towns and cities? Storming of her shores where so many more would perish? No. Negotiation between two heads of state was the only civilized way to handle this. Had England been more prepared, perhaps a fight would have been the necessary evil. Instead, they had proven too weak. Now they must gather what dignity that was left and ask for the best possible terms.

Ribbontrop and an interpreter met the British trio at the Berlin Templehof airport. Although cordial, the reception was cool. Ribbontrop did not waste time on formalities and ushered them to a waiting car.

The Reich's Chancellery was huge. As they drove through the gates and into the courtyard, Attlee wondered what kind of ego could build such a monstrosity. The building was gray and cold. From almost every edifice a large Swastika blew in the breeze. As the car came to a stop in the courtyard, a soldier dressed in a black uniform opened the door for them.

"Gentlemen. The Fuehrer wishes to begin discussions as soon as possible. You are prepared to represent your government in all negotiations are you not?" Ribbontrop asked while they walked through the door leading from the courtyard. Another black uniformed soldier held the door for them.

"As Prime Minister, I am authorized to negotiate on behalf of His Majesty's government. Of course any agreements we shall decide upon will be presented before the British Parliament for final consideration, but I assure you that whatever agreements we make, Parliament will back them."

Ribbontrop lead them and the interpreter up the large marble staircase and through a door to the tremendous red marbled hall of the Chancellery. Persian carpets and opulent wall hangings seemed dwarfed by the sheer size of the hall. A huge Eagle looked down upon them from the center of the far wall. Again the feeling of foreboding ran through Attlee. The building was designed to intimidate as well as display the riches of the Third Reich. The former was working on Attlee now and he could tell by their expressions, his companions felt the same.

Ribbontrop stopped before an enormous solid wood door. Another of the black uniformed guards stood to the side. Ribbontrop spoke to the guard. "The Fuehrer expects us. This is Prime Minister Attlee of England and his representatives. Please announce our arrival."

The Guard opened the door and stepped inside. Pulling himself to full attention with a click of his heels he announced their arrival.

Without waiting for a response the soldier turned to the group, bowed and said "The Fuehrer will see you now. Please enter."

He stepped aside and Ribbontrop strode into the office followed closely by Attlee, Eden and Halifax. Attlee looked at Eden and saw him role his eyes as if to say, "Do you believe this amateurish drama!" The guard had exited the room and closed the door making no noise. Hitler rose from his desk across the room, walked around and stood directly in front of it making no further move to greet his guests. He was dressed in a gray jacket with a swastika sewn on the left sleeve. He wore black slacks and brilliantly shined black shoes. Eden stifled a grin as he took in the picture of the little man trying to display a stern face.

Attlee noticed how barren the room was, and its sheer size making it seem more so. Besides the desk, there was a conference table with several chairs scattered around it, a map board, a bust of Fredrick the Great and two bookshelves. Above the desk, between to large windows, hung a portrait of Fredrick the Great. Large swastika flags draped the walls between the other large windows. He was a little surprised to see no one else besides an impeccably dressed older man with prinz-nez glasses standing to the rear of the desk.

The British delegation followed Ribbentrop as he moved directly in front of Hitler.

"Mein Fuehrer, Mr. Clement Attlee, Prime Minister of Great Britain, foreign minister Eden and former foreign minister Lord Halifax." Ribbontrop announced.

If the situation weren't so serious, Attlee would have laughed. The pair of them appeared idiotic in their attempt to act stately and professionally. Hitler appeared just as his caricatures in the English press had painted him. He immediately began to feel better about the negotiations, after all, how difficult could it be to out maneuver these two?

"Herr Hitler." He said bowing slightly and offering his hand.

Eyeing each of the British delegation separately, Hitler ignored the offered handshake and walked back around his desk.

Attlee was bewildered and he turned his head to look at Halifax and Eden. Halifax raised his eyebrows while Eden appeared to be studying the man.

As Hitler sat, he began: "Gentlemen, you are here at your own request. I assume your visit concerns a request for peace terms between our two nations. If that is not so, you may leave."

The older man standing beside Hitler apparently was the translator as he repeated what was said in English.

Attlee stifled the anger that had begun to rise in him and replied.

"Herr Hitler, I have come representing my…"

"Are you or are you not prepared to meet our demands?" Hitler bellowed, interrupting Attlee with a wave of his hand. He leaned forward onto his desk glaring at Attlee.

The translator, after a false start, repeated the question, bellowing in a fair imitation of Hitler.

"We have come to negotiate terms, yes."

"There will be no negotiations!" Hitler screamed. He reached for a set of documents on his desk and thrust them at Attlee. Attlee stood with his mouth agape.

"You will read and agree to the demands set forth in this document. After you have signed it, Herr Ribbentrop will give you a copy to bring to your people. If you refuse to sign it the consequences will be quite grave for your tiny island. I am prepared to unleash my full military might upon your nation and once and for all put an end to this war." Hitler declared, visibly controlling himself.

"Because of my understanding of the British people and our shared heritage, I offer you these terms. I do not wish to destroy the British but I will if you deem it necessary. Now Herr Ribbontrop will take you to an office where you may read the document." Hitler said as he sat back in his chair and picked up one of the papers on his desk. He put on a pair of spectacles that sat on the desk and began to read the paper, dismissing the delegation.

When the translator finished, Attlee was stunned. He was being dismissed like a servant! Did this man believe he could treat a representative of His Majesty's government this way?

"Herr Hitler, I came to negotiate a settlement to our differences, not to receive threats and demands!" Attlee's anger now came out full force in voice.

Hitler tore the glasses from his face as he rose from the desk. Leaning across it with both hands supporting him on the desk he said in a surprisingly soft tone: "Perhaps you do not understand or perhaps my translator does not know the correct words."

He glanced at the translator and glared back again at Atlee. The translator flushed and repeated the words.

"There will be no negotiations. You either accept my demands or return to your country and make what feeble attempts you can at preparing to defend against my armies!"

Hitler sat back down and picked up the paper again. He did not look up.

Attlee was appalled! This man understood nothing of diplomacy! The little man actually believed he could intimidate anyone and everyone!

"My god, so Churchill was right after all," he thought, "This is a madman!"

He was not prepared for this. He needed time. Turning to Ribbentrop he asked, "Where is this office? We need to study this document."

Without waiting for a reply he strode toward the exit where he waited, facing the huge door, his back to the room. Eden looked at Hitler and noticed he had carefully avoided looking up. He acted as if they were no longer worth his time. He glanced at Halifax and together they followed Attlee and Ribbontrop from the room.

"Right this way, gentlemen." Ribbontrop said as he opened the door and led them down the vast hall to a corridor on the right. Two doors down he stopped.

"You will find everything you need in here. If you require refreshments or are ready to return the document just press the button on the side of the desk. I will return to retrieve you and the document." He said as he opened the door and swept his arm into the room.

"Herr, Ribbontrop, that was the most embarrassing display of leadership I have ever seen! Does Herr Hitler not understand the principles of diplomacy among nations?" Halifax said as Ribbontrop turned to leave.

"The Fuehrer understands diplomacy much better than you it seems, Lord Halifax. We got where we are today because of your diplomatic

efforts. Czechoslovakia and Poland will attest to your mastery of diplomacy!" Ribbontrop sneered and walked away.

The three entered the office. It was small and sparsely furnished. In
the middle were an oak desk and chair, two chairs in front of the desk
and a desk lamp. Attlee walked over and sat at the desk. Eden thought
he looked like he was in shock. Halifax walked over to the desk, picked
up the document, took out his reading glasses from his coat pocket and
began to read.

Attlee looked up and sighed. It was then he noticed the large portrait
of Adolph Hitler that adorned the wall directly across from the desk.

"What has the lunatic set out for us?" he said to Halifax, staring at
the portrait.

Halifax read the demands. The first paragraph set the stage: "Within
72 hours after the signing of this agreement, England will cease all hostilities in regions under her control. All military leaders and civilian
representatives within these regions will turn administrative control of
these regions over to the nearest German Commander."

It went on to demand that all naval forces were to be returned to
England and prepared to be turned over to German authorities.
German authorities will be placed in control of all civil and military
forces within the British Isles and abroad. A German political advisor
will be appointed to assist in the administrative duties of foreign and
domestic responsibilities. The current British government could remain
in power provided the German political authority approved all policy
decisions. Oil and gold shipments from South Africa and the Middle
East will be shared between Germany and Britain, with seventy percent
going to Germany and thirty percent to England. All commercial shipping would be turned over to German authorities. All industry would
come under German control. War criminals as determined by the
German Government were to be arrested and turned over to German
authorities for trial in Germany. In return, Germany would not send an

occupying army. German civil authorities along with trusted British authorities would provide enforcement of all laws and policies.

Halifax removed his glasses and pinched the bridge of his nose as he finished reading and set the document on the desk in front of Attlee.

Eden looked at the two men and saw resignation.

"My God! If you sign this, Great Britain and the Empire will cease to exist! This is not an armistice, it is blackmail!" He shouted.

Attlee turned and looked at Eden. Eden saw resignation and sorrow in his eyes.

"What is the alternative? Further destruction and a loss that would result in even deeper enslavement? We failed to rally behind Churchill because we thought we could do better justice for the British people. It seems we will fail in that task." Attlee said, nodding to Eden.

"It seems we now have to make the hardest decision any of us will ever make. The survival of Britain rests on us." Attlee turned, putting his elbows on the desk. He bent and placed his head in his hands

Eden opened his mouth as if to protest then closed it. He realized Churchill's prediction was coming true and they were going to do nothing to prevent it.

Each man was lost in his thoughts for a moment, each thinking the same: How had it come to this? Ribbontrop's speech had spoken of a return to diplomatic relations, freedom from war for the British people. Having met the madman who ran the German machine, they knew that Ribbontrop had been used just as effectively as the bombs against their war weary nation.

Raising his head and glancing at the two men, waiting for some comment, Attlee's hand wavered over the pen on the desk. Without a word, Halifax retired to a corner of the room with his back to the other two. Eden turned from the desk and stared up at the portrait of the mad man.

Wiping a tear from his eye, shoulders slumped, Attlee reached for the pen.

CHAPTER 6

Harry was summoned to the White House late that evening. Earlier in the day, a messenger had brought a sealed envelope from Harry Hopkins. The envelope contained a short message from Hopkins stating that enclosed was a telegram the President wanted Harry to read and that the President would call for him and his answer later this evening.

Harry unfolded the telegram and read:

'Harry,

Forgive the presumptuous greeting. We haven't met but I assure you I know all I need to know about you. You have served His Majesty's government well these past months and I am quite sure you will continue to do so, no matter what the days and weeks ahead may bring.

I am writing directly to you with total disregard for chain of command for a very good reason. Mr. Roosevelt has informed me his government has made a proposal to you under my guidance. I urge you to accept their proposal. I can assure you, that while it is a bit out of the ordinary, it is fully within my capacity to order the turning over of military secrets when it is in our best interest. Believe me Harry; this is in our best interest. As Prime Minister, I assure you anything that you do at my request cannot be construed as treasonous.

Our nation faces it's gravest situation ever and we must do all we can to preserve the British peoples and her lands. I know you understand the situation as well as I and will do what is necessary to aid our country. Winston S. Churchill, PM'

"But you are no longer the PM, Mr. Churchill." Harry said to himself as he folded the telegram and placed it in his pocket.

#

Harry had been to the White House several times before on social occasions but had never been in the President's private quarters. As he stood in the hall outside the President's bedroom, He surveyed his surroundings. The White House looked every bit it's age. The carpeting was thread-worn in many places and the curtains on the windows he had passed were also worn.

"The Americans sure didn't believe in coddling their leaders!" Harry mused.

A light shown beneath the door of what, Harry knew, was called the Lincoln bedroom. Harry knew from his briefing on the white house that this was never Lincoln's bedroom, but had actually been his study. Mrs. Roosevelt now used it for her office.

The President's bedroom door open and a handsome woman stepped out, extending her hand to Harry.

"Mr. Lloyd, sorry to keep you waiting. My name is Missy, Missy LeHand. I am the President's secretary. He will see you now" The woman said as they shook hands.

Harry nodded and stepped into the room. The door closed behind him and he found himself alone in the room with the President of the United States.

The walls were covered with pictures. Most were of the president and other people but some were of ships and boats of various sizes. In the middle of the room Franklin Delano Roosevelt lie on a pillow laden bed. Pillows against the headboard propped up his back. He didn't have the famous cigarette holder clenched between his teeth, although Harry could smell the stale odor of tobacco.

"Harry! May I call you Harry?" The President asked as he motioned Harry to come to the side of the bed.

Harry nodded and stepped to the bedside. He was a little confused about protocol in this situation. As a diplomat, he had met many dignitaries and heads of state but never one in bed. As if reading his mind the president smiled and spoke.

"I'm sure the diplomatic schools you have attended didn't cover situations like this! Please, Harry, relax. I prefer informality even though it may offend your British sensibilities."

Roosevelt laughed and extended his hand.

Smiling and shaking his head, Harry reached forward to shake the president's hand. The president's grasp was powerful.

The President smiled and continued, " Harry, what we have asked you to do is very difficult for you I am sure. I know I would have very great difficulties if the roles were reversed. I have personally had the prime minister's message delivered to you. If you looked at the date of the telegram, you saw that he sent it while he was still Prime Minister. In my book it is still a valid order until countermanded by the current government. Since I don't believe anyone in the new government knows of its existence, I would venture to say that that is a highly unlikely occurrence. I am going to ask you to do as my friend has asked. Hand over to our government any war secrets that may be of value in our fight against Herr Hitler and his bully nation. You have been briefed on what, in particular, has our interest?"

Harry stared into the eyes of the President. The inflection in the President's voice had carried a degree of regret in having to ask such a thing and the Presidents face was relaxed and friendly but his eyes were hard and determined.

"Yes, Mr. President." Harry said continuing to look into the eyes of the President.

"However, what you wish to obtain is in England. I am assigned to the British delegation here."

The President shifted his gaze to the foot of his bed.

"Yes, well, I believe you will find that is not so in the morning. You see, Harry, we have filed a complaint with your foreign office." The President replied.

Harry raised his eyebrows but said nothing.

The President returned his gaze to Harry and continued, "We don't take too kindly to Nazi loving diplomats like you hanging around our shores with diplomatic immunity. We have even offered to transport your butt back to England ourselves!" Roosevelt's face broke into a wide grin.

Seeing the confused look on Harry's face, Roosevelt dismissed it with a wave of his hand.

"You need not worry son, your Ambassador Lothian has forwarded a glowing report on your performance of duties to the main office." Roosevelt winked at Harry.

The President's grin was infectious, and Harry found himself smiling back at the President despite himself. He understood the President's tactics and accepted it.

"I was told this morning that Prime Minister Attlee has signed an armistice with Germany. I am also told it does not favor Britain. How does this affect your plan, Mr. President?" Harry asked, realizing he really didn't care what affect it had. He had made up his mind. He would get the code machine for this man before the German's discovered its existence no matter what the cost may be.

"It makes your task more urgent." Roosevelt said, the grin dissolving into a more serious expression.

"It will take the Nazis some time to get their people in place and hopefully no one will the spill the beans before you have time to get the package for us. There are a great many people in your country that disagree with the armistice and are willing to help us out. Mr. Lothian has a list of names of the most prominent and of those in the best position to assist you. He will give you that list before you leave. I suggest you memorize it and destroy it before you arrive home."

"Will America still fight?"

"As long as I am President, I will do everything in my power to free the Nazi yoke from around the neck of Europe." The serious expression now replaced by one of determination.

"I have appointed Bernard Baruch to Chair the United States War Industries Board. He is a good man and will ensure our soldiers and airmen have the tools of war ready when the time comes. Conscription has bolstered our armies and air forces, and intense training is turning our boys into a fighting machine." Roosevelt said.

Settling back on the pile pillows that supported him, he continued, "Of course, I have an election coming up next month, which may change things, but I have faith in the American voters and I believe we can carry the day. There are places the mighty German army is vulnerable and we will attack those places as soon as it is prudent "

At that moment, Harry Hopkins bursting into the room waving a telegram followed a rushed knock at the door.

"Mr. President, I believe you will want to read this!" he said handing the paper to the President.

"Why Harry, you mustn't get so worked up! A man your age would do well to stay calm." The President chuckled as he took the telegram and began to read it.

The grin slowly faded from the President's face. He looked up at Harry and then to Hopkins.

"When did we receive this?" He asked

"A messenger from the Chiefs of Staff just delivered it. I think it is an answer to our prayers!"

"Could be Harry. Could be." Roosevelt replied thoughtfully then raising his head, "Have the Chiefs assemble in the Oval Office in an hour. We have some decisions to make."

The President reached for the bell rope used to summon his aide. Turning to Harry, Roosevelt handed him the telegram.

"We may have to arrange other transportation for you. It may be quite possible we won't be welcome in your homeland by tomorrow."

Harry frowned at the President and looking down, read the telegram. The telegram said the Germans had attacked and sunk an American destroyer that was escorting a British convoy to Iceland. All hands were lost. The U-boat had given no warning nor was there a request for identification.

Harry placed the telegram on the nightstand and left the room as the aides arrived. Harry Hopkins followed him into the hallway.

"Well, what do think now, Harry?" Hopkins asked as they both stopped in the hallway.

Harry looked back at the door to the President's bedroom then turned to Hopkins and asked.

"Will you declare war over this? Are you ready for war?"

"Ready or not, we have to play the hand dealt to us. I don't think we can afford to ignore this gift." Hopkins replied.

"It may be some time before the Germans provide us with such an opportunity again. Hitler could not have ordered this. We have had intelligence that he ordered hands off our ships until he settled with your country. I sure would hate to be that U-boat captain!"

Harry nodded and studied Hopkins for a moment. The man was visibly elated at the news. Hopkins was eagerly looking forward to war with Germany, Harry told himself. He hoped the rest of the Americans were ready.

"How does this affect my mission? It would appear to me that it is more important now than it ever was. Will I still have American support?" He asked.

Hopkins placed his arm around Harry's shoulder and replied, "Harry, you are our greatest hope now. If we declare war, Hitler will unleash his pack of U-boats onto our shores. It will cause immense problems for us until we can get the ships built and crews trained and in place to deal with them. If that code machine can give us the edge in knowing where and when they plan to strike, then it is vital we get our hands on it. I would go home and finish packing if I were you. I will try to get over and see you before you leave if time permits."

"Yes sir. I hope you people make the right decision. Whatever that may be. I'll do my best to get you what you need." With that, Harry headed down the hallway and to the stairs.

"Good luck and Godspeed Harry!" Hopkins said after him.

Harry was driven to his apartment at the British embassy where he began to pack. Things had changed drastically in the past week. His country had been devastated by the armistice and now it appeared as if the Americans would dive headfirst into the fray. Most of his colleagues at the embassy and even the ambassador had voiced their reluctance to return to England. There had been talk of the ambassador being replaced by a German diplomat, but after tonight that would not happen. Rumors had spread that Churchill intended to defy the government and setup a resistance movement in Canada. If this were true, when he finished this mission, he would go there and offer his services.

The dominions had so far not complied with the British demand to relinquish their control to the Germans. King of Canada, Menzies of Australia, Fraser of New Zealand, Smuts of South Africa, and Huggins of Southern Rhodesia had all turned their backs to Attlee. The British soldiers serving abroad had, to a man, renounced the armistice and joined the armies of the respective dominions.

Harry's mind reeled with questions: What kind of turmoil was the Foreign Office in England in? How much help could he really rely on? When would the Germans arrive? Would he have time to get in and get out?

The answers, Harry knew, would be known shortly. He also knew that this mission would answer what kind of man he was.

CHAPTER 7

Harry sat in the 'comforts' of the Catalina 'flying boat' staring out at the vast expanse of the ocean below. He had left Washington for Bermuda by a military transport plane before the sun had even risen. Hopkins did not see him off but had sent a messenger who handed him a note.

In Bermuda he had boarded the Catalina. The Catalina was not luxurious by any standards. He had to sit in webbed seats along the wall. After take-off he had read the note. The message from Hopkins gave instructions on how to contact the Americans once he was ready to be picked up with the package. It made no mention of whether the Americans intended to declare war. It ended with a bid for good luck.

Now, six hours into the flight, he had awoken from a much-needed sleep and tried to prepare himself for what lie ahead. He would land at Portsmouth and travel by train to London where he would meet with the new Foreign Secretary, Anthony Eden. Although Eden had been in the Churchill cabinet, Attlee had thought retaining him would help keep some of Churchill's foreign contacts, namely the Americans, on board. Harry had not been told how much Eden knew of his mission or if he knew of the request from Churchill. He would have to ascertain Eden's knowledge carefully. It was strange and troublesome to realize he had to now treat his own countrymen as if they were potential spies.

What should have been a pleasant homecoming was slowly turning into a nightmare.

#

Harry entered the customs office in Portsmouth carrying just one bag. He had shipped all of his excess clothes to his Aunt's' house for storage when he left Berlin. His father's sister had taken the London flat that Harry and his mother and father had shared when they lived in England. He would have to be careful not to involve her in anything while he stayed there. The custom's official reached for his bag but Harry pulled it away and handed him his diplomatic passport. The official inspected it then inspected Harry.

"Just a moment, sir" the official said and walked over to another man standing near the wall behind the counter.

Harry wondered what was going on. He knew he had not arrived in the usual way for diplomats, but the passport should have been enough for the minor official to pass him along.

The other man approached Harry.

"Mr. Lloyd? Your passport says you are a member of our Foreign Service. Why have you arrived aboard a neutral transport?"

"I have been recalled by my office and the fastest transport was the American Catalina out of Bermuda. Why does this concern you?"

"As you must surely be aware, Mr. Lloyd, we have signed an armistice with the Germans. Part of the stipulation of that armistice is that all diplomatic movements must be reported. You are not on the list."

"That is probably because I was just notified last night by urgent telegram. It must have been too late to add me to the list. Is this a problem?"

"No sir. I will keep your passport and forward it to your main office. They will notify you when you may pick it up again. Welcome back, sir" The official said as he retreated back to his position against the wall.

Harry eyed the two officials for a moment then picked up his bag and left the building. Taking a bus to the train station, Harry noticed the people seemed subdued. Even the elderly kept from their traditional gossiping. He did not see any officials on the bus or notice any law enforcement but it was if the passengers felt an eye was scrutinizing them. It was similar to what Harry had seen in Berlin.

As they approached London, the peaceful countryside gave way to the signs of war. Though the west end had escaped the worst of the bombings, it still showed signs of devastation. Blackened buildings stood next to burnt-out husks in more frequency as he approached the Charing Cross station. Harry saw rubble neatly piled into small hills on the street as he walked from the station; the same subdued looks on the passer-bys. Harry felt a deep sadness for his country and tried to avoid the sites by keeping his head to the ground as he headed for the foreign office building on Whitehall.

When Harry arrived at the foreign office he went to Eden's receptionist.

"My name is Harry Lloyd. I believe Mr. Eden is expecting me." Harry said.

The secretary looked up at Harry frowning, then a smile formed at her mouth. Harry guessed her to be near sixty years old. Grayed hair combed neatly into a bun on her head. She looked like one of hundreds of grandmothers.

"Harry! I don't suppose you remember me, but I once worked for your father. A marvelous gentleman he was too. My, that was ages ago! How are you?"

Surprised by her outburst, Harry mumbled "I'm fine, Mrs....?"

"Boatwright, Margaret Boatwright. Of course you don't remember! How silly of me! It's just that you look so much like your father, Well I apologize. Mr. Eden is expecting you. I will tell him you are here," She said as she rose from the desk, attempting to put the professional façade back in place.

It suddenly dawned on Harry. "No. Wait. It is I who must apologize, Mrs. Boatwright. It had been so long ago but I do remember you now. You worked with my father after he returned from India didn't you?"

Mrs. Boatwright stopped and walked toward Harry, taking his hands in hers. "Yes, it was right after my husband had been killed in an uprising there. Your father was kind enough to give me a job. Without it, I daresay, my life would have been much different. Your Aunt Agnes and I are dear friends. Does she know you are here?"

"No, I was hoping to phone her after my meeting with Mr. Eden. Until things settle a bit, I have no place to stay other than one of the foreign office's dreary apartments."

"I'll phone her while you are in the meeting. I'm sure she will be delighted to have you stay with her. She enjoys company so! Now let me tell Mr. Eden you are here and I'll ring up your Aunt." She said as she turned and walked down a short hallway. She knocked once on a door and entered.

Harry smiled to himself as his memory of Mrs. Boatwright returned. Now that he placed her in his memory he realized she hadn't changed much. She had always seemed elderly, or perhaps the correct word would be matronly, since he first met her as a teenager. The twenty odd years had added a little more gray to her hair but otherwise she looked the same. His father had given her a job out of respect for her husband but she had soon proven herself to be a very good secretary. She must still be, Harry thought, in order to gain the position she now held.

How many other people from his past life had he forgotten? Many of his father's associations he was sure. After his mother had returned to America, he had not had much contact with his father's social world other than occasionally meeting other members of the diplomatic corps who had known him.

Mrs. Boatwright returned. "Mr. Eden says to go right in. His office is the door on the left right down that hallway. It is so good to see you again, Harry" she smiled as she sat back at her desk.

The door was open and Harry entered the Foreign Secretary's office without knocking. He stopped just inside and tapped lightly on the door.

Anthony Eden rose from the desk and with a smile, walked over to greet Harry. He was dressed impeccably in a dark striped double-breasted suit. Harry noticed his mustache was well groomed, not a whisker out of place. Harry was struck by the fact that he was much younger than he appeared in pictures. In fact he wasn't much older than Harry himself.

"Mr. Lloyd, so glad you made it safely. How was your flight?" Eden said as he shook Harry's hand then turned to close the door. Up close Harry saw that the smile on Eden's face didn't reach his eyes. In his years of diplomatic service, he learned to view a man's eyes if you wanted to tell his true emotions.

"Please, sit down. I know you must be very tired." Eden said, pointing to one of the three chairs that stood in front of his desk. He returned to his desk chair and sat.

Harry sat in the middle chair, facing Eden.

"My first time in an airplane, but the flight was quite comfortable, sir." He replied.

"Yes, I hear the flying boats are a wonder." Eden said then leaned forward, elbows on his desk.

"Let's get right to it shall we? I know you need to get some rest. Do you mind if I call you Harry? I like to dispense with formalities." He paused and waited for Harry. Harry nodded his assent. Eden continued," How much do you know of the situation here?"

"Mr. Lothian kept us all pretty informed, but even he didn't know the particulars of the armistice before I left. I had a little taste of it at customs this morning."

"Oh? What happened?"

Harry told him of the incident.

"Yes, well, we haven't worked out the particulars of how we are going to follow the agreements laid out in the armistice yet. The official was a little over zealous. I'll have a talk with the Customs Secretary." Eden said as he waved his hand to dismiss the incident.

"I'm going to be frank with you Harry, the armistice is devastating to England. We are to become a puppet of the Nazis. Mr. Attlee cannot be faulted of course. The alternative would have been complete ruin of the British Empire."

Harry said nothing and Eden continued.

"Although no longer in office, I have a deep commitment to Mr. Churchill. I know of his orders to turn over any helpful intelligence to the Americans. No one else in the current government knows of this. Therefore we will need to be careful how we go about it. I can, through the powers of my office, assist you greatly. That is until the Nazi representatives get here. I believe we have only three or four days to get the Enigma machine - which is what it is called by the way-and the plans for the Turing Bombe out of the country. The Turing Bombe is the apparatus we designed to decipher the daily codes in order to figure the wheel combinations. As this device is quite large, the Americans will have to use our plans to reconstruct one themselves. The Enigma is not large, about the size of a typewriter. The plans are in tubes about two feet in length. There are four of them. Have you a plan?"

Harry had been watching Eden closely. He knew Eden had served His Majesty's government his whole adult life and had risen quickly in his field. He had been the youngest foreign minister ever appointed. Eden had obviously been well informed of his mission. His knowledge, however, could have come by many different ways. Lothian had spoke of possible government officials who were Nazi sympathizers. He had hinted that he believed they had engineered the push for an armistice. Harry didn't know how high up these officials went. Although Harry didn't feel as if he could trust anyone, his instinct told him Eden was trustworthy. Everyone was aware of the closeness of Eden and Churchill and Harry knew loyalty to Churchill meant anti-Nazi. Still, Eden was a politician. Harry decided he would not relinquish control of his mission to Eden or anyone else for that matter, no matter what their rank or position may be. Men like Eden were tools to be used.

"I will need to know where it is being kept. Not only the building, but also the room. I will also need transportation to Ireland. I believe Ireland will be the only route out of British Isles very shortly. Also I believe the Americans will be declaring war very soon and when that happens, they will no longer be allowed to land or embark from England." Harry said. His expression was impassive but his demeanor left no doubt as to his conviction. Eden raised his eyebrows but said nothing.

"I have a code, which I will use to contact the Americans when I have the package safely in my possession. Can our intelligence people be trusted? I may need to call on their resources." Harry finished.

Eden stared intently at Harry for a moment then relaxed and leaned back in his chair.

"I wouldn't let them in our secret, Harry. Word is the Nazis have already infiltrated many levels of it already."

"But doesn't that already compromise the Enigma secret?"

"No. Only the top two or three of the intelligence people know it exists. And I doubt if any of them have anything to do with the Nazis. Let me give you a run down on Bletchley Park. The place we keep the Enigma." Eden said as he placed his hands together as if in prayer.

"In August, code breaking operations were physically moved to Bletchley, about 40 miles from London. It was renamed the Government Code and Cipher School. It is currently under the direction of Naval Commander Alastair Denniston. Chess masters, mathematicians, professors and linguists were recruited from all over Great Britain to work there. Most came from Cambridge University.

"Denniston runs a tight ship. I don't question his loyalty or any of his subordinate officers. The problem may be in Military Intelligence. At least I suspect there may be a leak there. Some of our agents we had in France have already disappeared. Also, certain people knew word of Attlee's signing of the armistice before we even arrived back in England.

It would be best to use our own people as limited as their skills are in this sort of thing. I trust most of my people and I know many of them share our sentiments." Eden said.

Harry nodded as he absorbed the information.

"I can get you the material you need, maps, building layout and such. I'll have to do some snooping around to see what is the safest conduit into Ireland. As you can guess, the Irish aren't exactly broken up over what has happened here."

Harry managed a small smile at the mention of the Irish.

"I'm planning on staying with my Aunt Agnes while I'm here. You can have the material delivered there. Mrs. Boatwright knows the address. I think it would be best if we were not seen together too much in private. After all, I am supposed to be in your dog house, as the Americans say."

Eden smiled and placed his hands back on the desk as he moved forward in his chair.

"Yes, that was quite ingenious. I think our Intelligence fellows underestimate the deviousness of the Americans. I will spread the word you are under administrative leave, working under me until your allegiances are verified. In the end it may prove advantageous if the Nazis believe you are a sympathizer."

Rising from his desk and walking around the desk to Harry, he offered his hand. Harry stood and accepted it.

"I'll have the material delivered tonight. Guard it carefully and do take care, Harry. I was quite fond of your father and I would hate to think I may be responsible for injury or worse to his son." Eden said warmly then sensing apprehension in Harry, he added, "This is your show. Use me for whatever purpose you see fit. You may tell me as much or as little as you feel necessary."

Harry relaxed. His admiration for Eden was growing and he decided he liked Eden.

"Although this is new to me, I find it comforting to know I at least have a way to strike at the Nazis. I do think though, that you, Mr. Churchill and others of the former government may be in some trouble once the Nazis arrive. You may need care far more than I." Harry said as he turned to leave.

"That has been considered and I may need to take a special tour of the Dominions before they arrive. Poor Winston has been left without a passport and the King asked him to remain here." Eden said as he started to walk to the door with Harry.

Harry stopped and faced Eden.

"You mean he is not allowed to leave if he wishes?"

"That's the situation. Winston spoke of continuing the fight in his last speech before being replaced. The King and certain members of the current government feel he is a risk to the peace process. He has been ordered to remain here in England until the process is complete."

Harry outwardly showed concern as he said, "They realize of course that they have signed his death warrant. Hitler will never allow him to live. He is too much of a threat to their stability here."

"Our friends in government, even, I regret, the King are optimistic. They still fail to realize with whom they are dealing. I had my eyes opened on our little visit over there, and I know Mr. Attlee did too. He has aged considerably and seldom takes part in any proceedings anymore. He has even refused to relate to Parliament, his impression of the Nazi leader. However, it is too late to reverse our course. I am certain many members of the new government are actual Nazi sympathizers. Not a single protest was raised when the details of the armistice were read in chambers. Several of the old cabinet members left the chamber but none spoke for or against it. I myself have been shunned and ridiculed by my former friends for not having declined this position and for participating in the armistice talks, such as they were. After I had discussed it with Winston, it was decided it is better for one of us to still be able to get information and see first hand what is happening."

"Is Mr. Churchill under arrest or under guard?"

"No. He is free to come and go, although he hasn't left Chartwell since resigning."

Harry thought this over for a moment. "When will you see him again? Can you arrange for me to see him, say, this evening?"

"I visit him every evening. I'm sure he wouldn't mind if I invited you along. After all this is his idea you are working under. Why?"

"I'll explain to you both this evening. Is seven o'clock too late?"

"Heavens no. It is early for Winston. I'll pick you up at seven at you Aunt's."

"I'll see you this evening then." Harry said as he opened the door and exited.

#

Harry's old home was located on the far-west side of London in West Hampstead. The home, on Ajax Road, near the cemetery, was one of many look-alike homes built to accommodate the ever-expanding London population. His father had chosen this area because of its remoteness from the hustle and bustle of London center. He could see that it was also remote from the recent bombings. Very few signs of the devastation found closer to the city center was evident here. One or two homes appeared to have suffered minor fire damage and embers blowing in the wind most likely had caused this.

Although Harry had spent most of his youth here, seeing the neighborhood again did not make Harry nostalgic.

Most of the children he had known here, like him, had gone off to a myriad of private schools at an early age. Friendships were fleeting and not very strong. Not for the first time, Harry thought of how alone he had been and still was.

The government driver deposited Harry at the once bright blue house, now a dingy blue-gray hue.

Before Harry had the opportunity to knock, the white door was flung open. Harry's Aunt Agnes' forceful bear hug indicated how delighted she was to see him even before she mouthed the words. Agnes told him Mrs. Boatwiright had phoned and yes, of course, the house and his old room where his for as long as needed.

Agnes had been ten years older than Harry's father. Harry's mother usually described her as 'flighty'. She often would just up and leave to stay abroad with friends. Harry knew her as the Aunt that always brought presents. She was near seventy now. A blue-gray haired, (not much different in color than the house) plump woman, who was still 'flighty'. She couldn't sit still nor could she keep quiet. He had been inundated with her incessant chatter since he arrived: She didn't believe a word of the rumors that he was a Nazi sympathizer (Mrs. Boatwright must have told her.) She knew his father had raised his son to know better. Even the influence of his Catholic mother couldn't possibly have changed him so much. What did Harry think of the ruins of London? It was a good thing his father had chosen a district that was so far from the industrial heart of London. She had been quite safe here. No bombs had fallen anywhere near here. Oh sure they had plenty of air raid warnings but she didn't even bother going to the shelter anymore. Even when Mr. Tiddle the air raid warden, had threatened to report her. Why should she go into such a depressing stinking dirty hole when she was perfectly safe in her own home? Of course as a government servant if he felt it were more prudent that they did so, she would follow him. Did he plan on going to the shelter if an air warning sounded?

Harry explained to her that he didn't think any more raids would be occurring now that the armistice had been signed.

Oh, that horrible armistice! Would Harry give up his job to a Nazi? Would they be taking all the civil jobs? Did Harry know if they would cut off all their pensions?

Harry said he did not believe any of those things would happen and excused himself under the pretense of needing a shower and a bit of a nap. Agnes seemed to understand this and had left Harry on his own in his old room at the top of the stairs.

"I believe it would be safe to say no secrets would be safe with Agnes!" he said to himself, smiling, as he lay down on the bed. He had four hours until Eden would come to pick him up. He would take a short nap then shower and dress in time to meet Eden before Eden could be accosted by Aunt Agnes.

As Harry lie on the bed, thoughts whirled in his head. He had had an idea of how to accomplish the mission. The news about Churchill had changed things. There was no way he could leave the man to fate. He would have to deliver him, along with the code machine to the Americans. He already had a plan of getting to Ireland or the Scottish coast to be picked up by the Americans but he couldn't very well travel inconspicuously with someone as well known as the Prime Minister. He told Eden he would have something by tonight, but what? How did the famous move about so stealthily? He recalled a tale of how Roosevelt having gone fishing, while a double was used to roam the White House as if the President were still in residence. Would such a ploy work with Churchill? He didn't know, but it was a start.

Harry rose from the bed and checked the closet. Many of his clothes from a former life were there. Army uniforms and evening coats he had needed in Berlin, half a dozen or so old suits, and what he called 'muck about' clothes, old slacks and shirts worn purely for comfort. He knew most of these would still fit. He hadn't gained an ounce in the past five or six years. In fact he was probably more fit now. He had often spent time at the YMCA in Washington with young locals, playing basketball, a game a young staff lawyer at the White House had taught him, and swimming laps in the Olympic size pool. This had helped him relax in what was an often a pretty dull and frustrating assignment. His case he had brought with him contained his one new suit, underwear and socks as well as a shaving kit and other grooming essentials. These he placed in a drawer and into the small bathroom cabinet.

As he completed his tasks, he looked around the room. It seemed quite small now. As a child it had been his escape and he often turned it into an imaginary castle or an old American western fort where he would hold off Indian attacks. He smiled and sighed. The weariness began to overtake him and he returned to the bed.

He had dozed for a little over three hours. Showered and changed, he went downstairs to face his Aunt once again.

"I have made you a wonderful kidney pie Harry. It is so difficult these days to get meat but I have managed to save my rations. You must be absolutely famished!" she said as she flittered from the kitchen to the dining room, laying out two dinner places. "Let me just reheat it and we can dine and chat up a bit." She said as she headed back to the kitchen.

Harry eyed the dinner table and followed his Aunt. "I'm truly sorry Aunt Agnes, but I have to attend a meeting at the office this evening. I won't be able to join you I'm afraid. Although it does smell wonderful!"

Agnes held her hand to her breast and looked totally appalled as she said, "What can be so pressing that you can not take the time to eat properly? Why do they need you at this meeting? Don't they realize you have just arrived? A man should be allowed to rest before he is put back to the grind!"

"Its just part of the reason I have been recalled to England. With all that is happening, I am sure manners and etiquette may have to suffer some. Listen, why don't we have breakfast tomorrow morning? I don't know how late I'll be tonight but I'll make it a point to be up bright and early so I can start the day with you."

Agnes brightened a little and turned to shut off the stove. "Why that would be wonderful. Are you sure you won't want to sleep in tomorrow? After all you haven't had but a nap today and God knows when you'll get to bed tonight."

"I'll be there. It will help me get accustomed to the time change and give us a chance to catch up. Now if you don't mind I think I'll take a short walk while I wait for the car from the office." Harry leaned over and kissed his Aunt on the forehead. He was surprised to see her blush. He smiled at her and went to retrieve his coat.

The fall evening was chilly. It had been so long since he had been back to England and he would have to get use to the changes, especially the weather. This neighborhood, which once was animated with children from every household, was now quiet and except for a few dim lamps sneaking light through drawn shades, was completely dark. He imagined most of the folks who lived here now were elderly or that the children had been sent off to school as he had or off to the country during the 'Blitz'. It was strange, but he could not remember any of the names of his school chums from this neighborhood. He could see faces and remember laughter but names escaped him. Most of them were probably off serving in the Army or Navy. How many were now members of dominion armies he wondered?

As he passed an old brown house, he imagined old Mr. Thomas sitting on the steps, ready to entertain the neighborhood kids with tales of past adventures. Mr. Thomas had spent his life as a sailor and had visited many fascinating far-of exotic places. Harry used to enjoy listening to the stories of half-naked natives and pirates who roamed the seas. He wondered what had happened to Mr. Thomas. He must surely be dead by now. There were no signs of life in the old house to suggest otherwise. As Harry turned to retrace his steps back to the house, he saw headlights approaching. The dark sedan pulled to the curb near him and the back door opened.

"Thought that was you. Get in Harry, Winston expects us." The voice of Anthony Eden came from the car interior.

Harry glanced about the street, noticing a few black out curtains had moved to reveal small slivers of lights emitting from a few of the houses. He thought an automobile must be a strange sight here since the war started as he entered the sedan. Instinct told him he must remember that,

Eden had handed him a package as soon as he had settled in the seat. Eden reached over and pulled curtains that hung on the side widows and motioned for Harry to do the same on his side. He then snapped on a small lamp that hung from the front seat.

"Those are the items you requested. There is even a blueprint and a photo of the Enigma machine. External security has been lessened at Bletchley Park, the place where the machine is stored, so as not to draw any undue attention to the place. Internal security is still pretty tight, but with a letter from me, I'm sure you will be able to get access without any problems. How you extract the machine and plans from the place is up to you." Eden said.

Harry quickly looked over the photographs of Bletchley Park and the machine. It was not much bigger than a typewriter as Eden had said, but it was too big to fit in a standard case. Harry noticed that there were many fabricated buildings all around the main building."

"What are the other buildings?" he asked.

"That's where all the chess masters, mathematicians, professors and linguists work. Churchill truly believed these people could crack any code. He was right. These eggheads, as I call them, have cracked many of the other codes the Germans have used besides the Enigma. Though some codes have taken weeks even months to crack. Each hut has a different responsibility; naval codes, air force codes, diplomatic codes and so forth are assigned to different huts. You will not have to worry about those buildings. The Enigma is located in the cellar of the main building. The Enigma wheels and Turin Bombe plans are kept in a vault next to the room housing it, I'm told."

"How do you keep it a secret with so many people working there?"

"Strict security rules are in effect. People in building 3 do not know what people in building 4 are doing, and so on. They all have different working schedules and are housed in private residences all around the village. They do not have time to socialize or interact with anyone but people assigned to their own sections.

"The number of persons allowed to receive Enigma messages is strictly limited. An officer personally delivers messages to the commander, and destroys them after they are read. Messages are not retransmitted or repeated. No one who has knowledge of Enigma is allowed to get himself in a position where he might be captured. In other words, Bletchley is their home for the duration. Unfortunately that duration has been significantly shortened." Eden added as he looked down at his hands. Harry could tell the armistice was a painful thought for him.

Eden looked back up and continued.

"Everyone thinks the main building is administrative only. And for the most part, it is."

"Sounds pretty secure, but you would think something like this would leak out. I know if I knew of its existence and its value to the war effort and I was a lowly 'egghead' as you say, I would sooner or later tell a colleague, just for the lack of anything else to talk about."

"The eggheads don't work on the machine. Although deciphered messages travel around the place, handpicked military intelligence officers are the only ones allowed near it. There is perhaps, five or six if these fellows. They are being transferred tomorrow to Northern Ireland on a pretense of needing to keep an eye on the Irish while the Germans move in. The cellar will be free of personnel and you will have authorization to visit the cellar. The commander at Bletchley has been told of your visit, although he has not been told of your mission. As I said earlier, we believe him to be a solid character, but the fewer that know the better."

"How do you explain a minor diplomat visiting an intelligence center?" Harry asked.

Eden's face brightened in the dim light of the lamp. Reaching into his coat pocket he said, "Oh, yes I forgot. As of today, you have been reassigned to MI5, the intelligence service, at the request of the Germans. That entitles you to a promotion, which I have had endorsed for you. Congratulations, Colonel!"

He handed Harry a small leather case. Harry opened it and found the official seal of British Intelligence staring back at him from his new badge.

"At the request of the Germans?" Harry asked, a bit surprised.

"Yes. Of course the Germans know nothing about you and did not really request the move, but it fits with your Nazi sympathizer cover, don't you think?"

Harry felt Eden was enjoying this. He put the box into his own coat pocket.

The car swung left and began slowing.

"Will my raise be in British pounds or Reich marks?" He asked as he put the photos back in the envelope and reached over to shut off the lamp. Although he couldn't see him, Harry could hear Eden chuckling next to him.

Churchill's butler, Inch, led the pair upstairs into the study where Churchill was sitting in a lounge chair near a glowing fireplace. He was dressed in what Harry believed to be a maroon silk smoking jacket with black pajama pants and blue slippers. He had a snifter in one hand and his famous cigar in another. He struggled to rise from the lounge and, giving in to the futility of it, set his snifter down on a side table and with a broad sweep of his arm, motioned for them to sit anywhere.

"Ah! It is good to see you again, Anthony. The Empire still survives I take it?" Churchill smiled at Eden.

Eden smiled and made a mock bow.

"And you sir, must be Mr. Lloyd. Harry I believe. Please call me Winston. No need to stand on ceremony here. Would either of you care for a drink? I have some wonderful Hine Cognac here or I can have Inch bring some coffee?"

Eden said he would join Winston in some cognac. Harry shook his head. He was a bit awed being in the presence of the man, although he found his appearance to be under whelming. It was the voice and the famous cherubic face that struck Harry as awe-inspiring. His speeches and picture had been seen and heard all around the world in the past year and had inspired many a British citizen.

Eden strode over to the cabinet near the wall and took out another snifter. He then walked over and poured from Churchill's bottle. He remained standing near Churchill's chair.

Harry noticed the bottle was nearly empty and he eyed Churchill carefully.

"I can see by the look in your eyes, that you believe the terrible stories about my drinking habits, don't you Harry? Don't worry, son, this is my first glass of the evening. When it comes to business, I prefer to be wide awake and sober." Churchill said grinning around the cigar he had promptly put in his mouth. "Although, of late, many believe I have been neither!"

"I have briefed Harry, Winston. As I said on the phone this afternoon, Harry wishes to speak to us on another matter. Isn't that right Harry?" Eden said as he took a drink of the cognac.

"Yes, sir. Mr. Churchill."

"Call me Winston, Harry, please." Churchill said with mock consternation on his face.

"Yes, well, Mr. Eden told me of your situation here. I think you ought to go out with the Enigma machine and plans when we leave. You will surely be in great danger once the Germans arrive."

"I know Herr Hitler has his plans for me as well as other members of the war cabinet that had opposed him, but my ugly mug is quite known you know. I believe it would be rather difficult for me to travel."

"I don't believe so. Anthony has told me you haven't left Chartwell since your resignation. That means people have become accustomed to believing this is where you always are. I'm sure you must have had or at least considered a double while you were in office. President Roosevelt has one and I know Hitler has used one on occasion. He can be used as a decoy."

Winston looked up at Eden who at the same time looked at Churchill. Both turned and looked at Harry simultaneously.

"I did have such a man. A minor actor on a London stage. What do you propose?" Winston said as he leaned forward, intently gazing at Harry.

Harry told him of his plan. When he finished he watched Churchill closely. Churchill sat back and blowing a puff of smoke towards the ceiling, seemed to be considering the plan. After a minute he turned to Harry.

"You know Harry, that may just work! I have been brooding here since my dismissal about how I could get out and carry on the struggle. Your simple plan may just be the answer. What do you think Anthony?" He asked as turned his head up to Eden.

"I believe it will work, Winston. I can find the actor I'm sure. I think he would be delighted to be back on the payroll again. He isn't all that great an actor, Harry." Eden added, looking over to Harry. "I don't believe I'll mention the suspected German intentions to him though. He may not like that part much." Eden said as he walked over to sit on a sofa near Harry.

"Wonderful! Now tell me Harry, what is your plan for getting the Ultra for our friends?" Churchill said as he settled back and reached for his snifter.

Harry looked at Eden confused.

"Ultra is the code word Winston uses for the Enigma machine." Eden answered his unspoken question. "He is a bit of a fan of code words aren't you Winston?'

"They serve their purpose. Any little thing that confuses the enemy or gives them pause is valuable. By the way, Harry, for our little escape plan, you can refer to me as Colonel Warden. It's a little pseudonym I use when I want to keep my name out of the headlines."

Harry nodded then told them of his plan to get the Enigma. His plan would require a lorry and driver as well as some explosives. Could they help in getting them?

"Of course. Anthony, you will see about the lorry won't you?" Churchill asked as he looked to Eden. Leaning forward in the lounge, he turned back to Harry.

"You have a knack for constructing brilliant but simple plans, Harry. You may well just be in the wrong business!"

"Yes, sir. The plans are simple but I believe they will work. The only thing needed would be some sort of explosive that I could easily carry in with me and won't make too much noise."

"We have a relatively new weapon that is similar to putty. The scientists call it RDX. The military calls it plastic explosive. Ironically, it was actually invented by a German fellow just before the turn of the century. You can mold it into shape and use as little or as much as you need without carrying around bulky sticks of dynamite and fuse wires. If you were to set it off behind or under something that could muffle the explosion, I think it would be perfect. It is quite safe. I hear you can burn it, shoot it and even run over it with a lorry and nothing will happen. But hook this stuff up to a blasting cap!" Churchill emphasized an explosion by slowly raising his hand above his head as he wagged his hand. He chuckled and turned to Eden. "Anthony, you can obtain some of this can't you?"

"I can try. I'll find some excuse or another to obtain it. I'll get it first thing in the morning."

"Perhaps tonight would be best. I'll call Dill myself after you leave and have him deliver the stuff to your home. And for God's sakes Anthony, don't blow yourself up before you can get it to Harry!" Winston chuckled again as he uttered this last remark.

Eden smiled as he raised his snifter and drank. Both of the gentlemen were smiling broadly with a twinkle in their eyes. Harry couldn't help but think how much like a child the former Prime Minister was, instead of a promise of candy, a little excitement and intrigue was all that was needed to light up his life. Harry hoped he could keep him entertained and keep his ass alive at the same time.

It was near midnight when Eden dropped Harry off at his flat. Eden left with the promise he would send the lorry and driver around his place whenever he decided he needed it. Things seemed to be moving along a lot smoother than Harry had anticipated and he had feeling his mission was going to be quite successful. He wondered what the Americans would make of Churchill accompanying the package but he was sure Roosevelt would welcome him.

Lost in his thoughts, Harry hadn't noticed the car parked up the street. As he approached his door, a figure stepped from the shadows.

"Mr. Lloyd?" The figure spoke.

Harry, surprised, stepped back and assumed a defensive stance he had learned in the army. His senses were on full alarm now. He hadn't really considered the danger involved but now his mind whirled with all sorts of possibilities. He didn't sense aggression in the man, yet the circumstances were suspicious.

"Who are you?" He asked.

"I'm a friend. I have been sent to invite you to visit with another friend." The man said stepping forward into the dim moonlight.

Harry could make out a young man, over six feet in height, dressed as if he worked the docks, and powerfully build. The image didn't fit the voice or the speech. The man had a slight cockney accent but it was barely perceptible. Each word was pronounced with precision. The man was more than a simple goon, Harry guessed.

"I do not believe we have met, therefore I don't believe we are friends." Harry said as he straightened and glanced about for a good escape route, if the need arose.

The man watched Harry glance from side to side then spoke: "Mr. Lloyd, there is no cause to be alarmed. I mean you no harm. Our mutual friend had learned you were back in England and asked if I would fetch you so he and you can have a chat."

"Who is this mutual friend?" Harry said, relaxing a bit more but still wary.

"Lord Mosely, sir."

Harry recalled the name. Lord Oswald Mosely, ex-member of Parliament, was the leader of the British Fascist Union; Vehement anti-Semites. The British version of the Nazis. Harry had heard he and a bunch of other fascists were to be arrested. I guess with the Germans coming to town, someone had thought better of it.

"What does he want with me? I'm a minor official in the Diplomatic Corps. And my politics are apathetic if anything."

"He didn't say. Lord Mosely just asked me to fetch you. That's all."

"And if I refuse?"

"Then I am to go and tell him you refused."

"That's it? Just tell him I refused?" Harry asked, surprised.

"That's it sir. Now will you come with me or do I tell him you refused?" the man asked, stepping towards then around Harry. He continued several steps down the path.

"What the hell would Mosely want with me?" Harry thought then replied, "I may as well see what the gentleman wants. Where are you to take me?"

"Not far. He has taken residence near here to escape the bombing. We could walk, but it will be much faster driving."

"It's late already. Let's go." Harry said as he followed the man up the street to his car.

As they approached the car, Harry remembered what he had noticed about cars on this street earlier. "You have got to start paying better attention, Harry, or you won't last long in this game!" he said to himself.

CHAPTER 8

The man, whose name was George, Harry had learned on their short drive, led him into the small flat. It was a mirror image of the hundreds of flats in this neighborhood and Harry could have traversed it with his eyes closed. He was led into a small den where the man he recognized as Oswald Mosely stood, smoking a cigar. He was dressed in a smoking jacket, ascot and dark pants. Harry got the impression the man was trying to imitate some sort of motion picture star.

Mosely turned and walked over to Harry and shook his hand.

"Glad you could make it, Mr. Lloyd! I hope George was polite enough. He has a tendency to act rather brutish at times." Saying this, he dismissed George with a wave of his hand. George left the room closing the door behind him.

"I know the hour is late, but could I interest you in a drink?"

"No, thank you sir. I would like very much to get on with why I was brought here. As you say, the hour is late." Harry said, staring at Mosely.

"Quite. Well I'll be brutally honest and get straight to the point. Are you one of us, Mr. Lloyd?" Mosely asked, narrowing his eyes and cocking his head in anticipation of Harry's answer.

"One of us?" Harry asked. "He has heard the Nazi sympathizer story and believes he can recruit me!" Harry said to himself.

"Yes. Us, meaning the enlightened Englishman whom sees the enemy not as Germany, but as Jews and Bolsheviks, Mr. Lloyd. We believe

Hitler is a far cry better leader to have than Winston Churchill and his self-serving pack of lies. You understand now don't you?" Mosely walked over and sat on one of two chairs in the room and motioned for Harry to take the other.

Harry didn't move.

"What makes you believe I have the same sentiments as you?" Harry asked.

"We have eyes and ears in many different positions in government. They have told me how the Americans treated you. Banishing you from their hallowed shores as if you were some sort of criminal. All because you have showed some sympathy for Adolph Hitler. Come now, Mr. Lloyd, here in my home you have nothing to fear. You may speak honestly."

Harry realized this was an opportunity to get a little more insight into Hitler's machine here in England. He doubted even military intelligence had an insider to this group. As important as that was his mission came first, he would have to play it careful.

"My political views are just that; my political views. I don't make it a point to share them with strangers. Especially strangers with your reputation."

Harry saw an instant of anger flare up in Mosely's eyes.

"Mr. Lloyd, you believe the government rumors? I stand for the same ideals as you. I am loyal to the Empire. As loyal as you, Mr. Lloyd." He said stabbing a finger in Harry's direction. He took on a far away look in his eyes and Harry could see him puff up as if addressing his friends.

"I have served my country faithfully. I fought in the last war and have served in Parliament. I'm no traitor, Mr. Lloyd. I may perhaps have a different perception of our beloved country. We suffer from our success. Our social order remains intact but this has caused a wide gap between the haves and have-nots. Men are breaking their backs to earn a wage that hardly pays to keep his family fed. The depression didn't help. Our unemployment is at an all time high.

"On the other hand, look at Germany. Just ten years ago, Germans needed wheelbarrows full of reichmarks to pay for a loaf of bread; her borders violated by occupying forces. The government was weak and ineffectual. Now, Hitler has rescued the economy, regained her rightful lands and Germany has the lowest unemployment in all of Europe.

"If it is wrong that I wish to see the Empire as strong or stronger than it ever was, then I am guilty. I believe we can rise above our social and economic doldrums by emulating the methods of the Germans. Surely, you see the logic in this?"

Harry shook his head.

"I know the speech Mr. Mosely. I read Goebbel's propaganda too. My question is what do you intend to do now? Germany has won. We will soon see her representatives at all levels of government right here in England. Are you to be one of her puppets in government?"

Mosely's anger became more glaring. His face was crimson and his eyes were hard as steel.

"I am no one's puppet! I have fought for what is right for England and it just so happens it coincides with what is right for Germany. If the Fuehrer wishes to reward that fight that is his choice. I do not ask for any favors Mr. Lloyd!"

Harry shrugged. He realized he was dealing with a man who had fallen between the cracks of rational and irrational. Mosely was mad. How mad he didn't know but he knew Hitler's henchmen wouldn't rely on him for anything important. He was wasting his time.

"Mr. Mosely, whatever direction I have chosen to send my loyalty, I have no need for you or your people. Our differences are too clear. So, in answer to your first question, No. I am not one of you. Now if you'll excuse me it is late. I have work to do in the morning and I must get some rest." Harry said as he turned and opened the door.

"If you believe we are just amateurs playing a game Mr. Lloyd, you are mistaken! You will see when the Germans arrive. It is people like you who will suffer! They need people who are organized and loyal, not people who play at fascism! You'll see!" Mosely raged.

Harry closed the door on Mosely's ranting. George stood in the hall. He shrugged, slipped on his gloves, and led Harry out to the car. As they drove the short distance to his home Harry thought to himself, "No wonder the world is in such turmoil. Old fools and psychopaths all fighting to be King!"

CHAPTER 9

Harry kept his breakfast appointment with Aunt Agnes as promised. He didn't know what the rest of the day would bring but if all turned out as he planned, he'd be on his way back to the United States in a couple of days.

While they caught up on old times, a message arrived for Harry. It was telegram from his mother. She hoped his journey went well and that Agnes was in good health. Then cryptically, she mentioned that his Uncle Sean O'Hara would love for him to come and visit him while he was home. Uncle Sean was Harry's grandfather's much younger brother in Ireland. He had not heard of him in at least twenty years and had never met him. Why had his mother mentioned him so suddenly? He stuck the telegram in his pocket and went to help Agnes with the dishes.

"Good news I hope." Agnes said when he joined her at the sink.

"A telegram from mother. She hopes my trip went well and asks after you." He smiled as he picked up a towel.

"She mentions me?" Agnes seemed surprised. "Your mother and I haven't spoken since your father's funeral. To tell you the truth, Harry, we didn't get along so well. If we hadn't both loved your father, I doubt if we would have even spoken civilly to each other. I am not fond of her heritage."

"Mother never spoke of Irish–English relations in her life. I don't think she ever gave it much thought." Harry said, reaching for a plate. "You hid it well. I would have never guessed you disliked her."

"She was married to your father and he loved her. I would never interfere in that. I made polite conversation when we were together and your mother did the same."

"They did raise me in the Protestant faith you know. Mother even took me to church when father was away."

Handing Harry another dish, Agnes replied, "Did she now? I never knew that. Well, perhaps the old girl wasn't so bad after all!" She smiled up at him and changed the conversation.

"What will you be doing today? Are you going into the office?'

"Yes. In fact, I'll be leaving shortly. I have some things I need to catch up on."

"I can imagine with the Germans about to land, it must be quite busy."

"Yes, that has people jumping. More in wonder of what their coming will bring than anything else." Harry said putting the last of the dishes into the cupboard and setting the towel on the counter.

"I enjoyed our time together this morning Aunt Agnes. It's good to catch up on old times. It's been so long since I have been around family. We must do it again." He bent and kissed her on the forehead. "I have to change and get ready to go into the office. Does the underground still run?"

"Yes, into the city center but I hear things aren't so easy if you go east." She replied as she undid her apron.

"I enjoyed it too Harry. We have lots of mornings to catch up now don't we?" She asked with slight worry in her voice.

"Until they assign me elsewhere." Harry said as he walked from the room."

"Or until the Germans take you." Agnes said to his retreating back.

\#

Harry left the underground at Westminster station and head lowered to the wind. He proceeded west to King Charles Street and up Horse Guards Road to the foreign office building.

Harry found Mrs. Boatwright at her station and asked if Mr. Eden was available.

"He has someone in with him at the moment, but I'll tell him you are here." She said as she rose from the desk, walked down the hall, knocked once and entered the foreign secretary's office.

"Mr. Eden says to go right in." She said when she returned. "Are you and Agnes having a good visit?" she added.

"Thank you. Yes. It has been quite pleasant so far." Harry said as he started down the hall.

The door had been left open and Harry entered the office. Eden was at his desk and another gentleman was seated in one of the leather chairs across the desk.

"Harry! Come in. Sit down." Eden said from behind his desk, pointing to one of the chairs next to the other man.

"I would like you to meet Bill Donovan." Eden said. Donovan stood and shook Harry's hand and introduced himself as Bill. Harry nodded at the man and both sat down.

Eden continued, "Bill has been over here as an unofficial observer for U.S. Secretary of the Navy, Frank Knox. He doesn't tell us what he is observing, but we pretty much give him full run of the place." He smiled at Donovan.

"Mr. Donovan has had some special contact with our people in MI5 and MI6. Seems part of his assignment is to study our intelligence methods. Isn't that right Bill?"

Donovan cleared his throat, "Yes sir." Reaching inside his coat pocket, he took out an envelope and handed it to Harry.

"This telegram came this morning by special courier from the embassy. Since I don't know where you are staying, I came to Mr. Eden to deliver it. Go ahead and read it. It might help explain some things.

Harry opened the envelope and with a glance at Donovan and Eden, he began to read:

'Harry,

I received reports that you have arrived safely. I am relieved to know that. I also understand you have met with Mr. Eden and Mr. Churchill. Winston is quite impressed with you. He says your plan for obtaining the package is simple but brilliant. I have every faith in your abilities. I especially admire your determination in helping Winston escape the Nazi talons. However, I must emphasis that this must not jeopardize the original mission. Winston is a dear friend and I would do everything in my power to ensure his safety but one man cannot compromise the safety of millions that are at stake here.

Mr. Hopkins contacted your mother the day you left. He did not mention your true mission, but hoped to alleviate any anxiety she may have over your 'deportation'. Harry assured her that any accusations she may hear are false.

Your mother is a marvelous woman, Harry. She understood completely and did not ask for details. She volunteered the name of a relative of yours that may be in a position to help. He is in Ireland and your mother is going to notify him to expect a visit from you soon.'

That explains Uncle Sean, he thought to himself and continued to read.

'Harry forwarded a telegram to you from your mother through our embassy there. I hope you have received it.

I have authorized Mr. Bill Donovan to give you any and all assistance you may require. As you are well aware, the Irish and you British do not have the best of relationships and Bill can help smooth the way. At your discretion, please use Bill and his resources. He has accomplished more for us over there than even your government knows. He can explain better than I can.

Good luck Harry. Please remember that the package is your primary mission.

Franklin D. Roosevelt.'

Harry folded the letter, placed it back in the envelope and shoved it into his coat pocket.

"Seems we are to be working together, Mr. Donovan." Harry said.

"Yes. It's Bill by the way. Although I have not read your letter, I am sure it helps explain my presence. I hope that does not interfere with your plans. I will be acting mostly as a source of information and in some cases, an intermediary, for you. You run the show."

Harry turned to Eden. "You are aware of what my message says?" He asked.

"No. But Bill says it comes from the highest sources, that is enough for me. Just let me know if there are any changes to our plans." Eden replied then reached behind his chair.

"Here is the item we discussed last night. Having seen it, I find it hard to believe it is so deadly. Looks quite harmless actually." He said as he handed Harry two small boxes about the size of a cigarette pack.

Donovan looked at the boxes. "Plastic explosives?" he asked Harry.

"Yes. How did you know?"

"I've seen the official nondescript boxes before. If you folks intend to hide its contents, you really should use more imagination in packaging." He said as he looked over to Eden.

"Thanks. I'll tell our military officials your suggestion." Eden said frowning.

"Now Harry, perhaps you should fill Bill in on your plan. Perhaps you can find a place where you will not be disturbed. It is a nice morning; I suggest St. James Park across the street. I'll stop around tonight, Harry, to see if there are any changes I should bring to Winston." He said as he rose from the desk.

Harry placed the boxes in his coat pocket, one on each side. Again he admired Eden's instincts. He had rightly deduced that there were some things that he and Donovan needed to discuss that he shouldn't be privy to.

Harry and Donovan stood, shook Eden's hand and left the building.

They found a bench in the park and sat down.

"The sandbags don't do much for the exterior decoration do they?" Donovan said as he pulled his coat closer together and crossed his legs. He nodded in the direction of the foreign office building. Sandbags had been stacked ten feet high in front to protect from damages by bombs.

Despite the brilliant sunshine and the calming of the wind, the air had a chill to it. Harry noticed the trees had begun to lose their leaves and there was a red and orange blanket at the foot of the trees.

"It is a cold reminder of what my country has had to endure these last few months. If Attlee hadn't signed the armistice, I believe today would have been a good day for the Luftwaffe." Harry said looking up to the cloudless blue sky. Barrage balloons still floated above the city as another reminder.

"Oh, they would have loved this weather all right. I imagine the tubes would have been full of huddled scared masses today."

"What exactly is your function Bill?" Harry asked, still looking skyward, imagining the dogfights that had occurred there.

"For the most part, I observe your Navy's tactics in fighting the U-boat menace. Send reports to Secretary Knox and pass on to your officials any questions he may have." Donovan said as he watched some pigeons searching for food on the ground. Life was hard even for the birds, he thought to himself. Few people had bread to spare even for the pigeons.

Harry looked across the street at the treasury building and the foreign office building next to it. Sandbags nearly covered the whole ground floor of both buildings.

"There must be more. The President seems to think you have contacts and resources to lend to my mission. How is it an American without portfolio could have such things available to him?" Harry asked.

"I also perform some tasks for the President. He is concerned at our lack of overseas intelligence gathering abilities. He has asked me to observe your intelligence services' methods. I have a contact in MI5 that

wishes very much for us to enter the war. He has been exceedingly helpful." Donovan said, uncrossing his legs and leaning forward on the bench.

"I see. How much do you know of my mission?" Harry asked.

"I know you weren't deported for the reasons that have been spread
around. In fact you weren't deported at all, but returned to England to
help us obtain some sort of intelligence information. I know the
President and Mr. Churchill are involved. I also know that you may
require the services of the Irish Republican Army, which is quite
intriguing in itself."

"I didn't plan on using the services of the IRA, but the more I think
about it, it is probably a good idea." Harry said glancing over at
Donovan. He continued to tell Donovan the particulars of his mission
and his plans for accomplishing it.

"Sounds plausible enough." Donovan said, nodding.

"The only problem I see is in getting Churchill out. He is a pretty big
package to transport about, not to mention quite recognizable. I don't
believe the Irish will take too kindly to his presence either."

"The President expressed similar concerns in his letter. I cannot leave
him behind though. His options are limited and I know the Nazis will
kill him if they get their hands on him. I will get him out, one way or
another, without compromising the primary mission. How much do
you know about Bletchley?"

"I know it has a ton of security in and around it. I know it is a code-
breaking center. I have been there to pick up intercepts concerning
German naval operations. I also know that a barge carrying troops pre-
viously assigned there, blew up and sunk last night shortly after leaving
Stranraer on its way to Ireland. I don't believe in coincidences." He said
as he turned and looked at Harry.

Harry's head jerked around to Donavan at the mention of the sinking. "What caused the sinking?"

"Don't know. Fellows at MI5 blame the IRA. Some think it was a U-
boat. Personally I think it was your own folks. It is kind of convenient

don't you think, that the only group to work in the cellar, where I believe your device is kept by the way, should happen to die?"

"Are you suggesting the government had them killed? Preposterous! No one in the present government, outside of Eden knows of the device." Harry said incredulously, then added, "You aren't thinking that Anthony had anything to do with it do you?"

"No. Anthony doesn't wield that kind of power. His old boss does though." Donovan said looking up at Harry.

"Churchill? I don't believe he is capable of such a monstrous thing." Harry said shaking his head.

"He's a politician; A very successful politician. To him soldiers are tools to be used. He doesn't put faces on them when he issues his orders. He just uses them. He has the responsibility to weigh all the consequences and must act on the best method of accomplishing his goal. In this case, burying the existence of the device you seek. No one is left to talk once the device is gone."

Harry pictured Churchill as he had seen him last night. He tried to picture him they way Donovan now painted him. Although he knew that what Donovan said made sense, he couldn't reconcile the two images of the man. Harry could be cold and calculating when the need arose but he didn't know if he could order the deaths of innocent men. Given the circumstances, he had to accept Churchill could.

Harry turned away from Donovan, looking at the western end of the park where two couples sat near the pond, enjoying the sunshine.

After a heavy silence, Harry turned again to Donovan. Donovan was rubbing his throat and had an intense look of concentration on his face.

After a moment, Donovan spoke.

"You'll have to be careful with that plastic explosive. Too much and you'll bring the place down around your ears." He reached down and picked up a handful of dirt.

"This much, if placed next to a support beam, will drop the building on top of you." He then poured most of the dirt from his hand. "This small amount, if covered with paper, cardboard or rags and placed near an outside wall should do what you want." He again reached down, this time grabbing a small twig. "This is the primer, Harry. It is like a lighter. Push the pointy end into the explosive like this." Donovan demonstrated by pushing the stick into the small pile of dirt in his hand.

"Twisting the top of the primer will start the ignition process. Depending on the primer you have been given it could be set for any where from five minutes to an hour." He brushed the dirt and stick from his hand, put both hands in his coat pockets and sat back.

Harry reached into his pocket and without removing it, opened the box. He felt a clay-like substance. He closed the box and reached into his other pocket. This time he extracted a small pencil-like item. He handed it to Donovan. Donovan withdrew his hands from his pocket and examined the tube.

"You'll have a short time on this one. It's a five minute fuse." He said, handing it back to Harry. Harry slipped it back into his pocket.

"Seems they have more faith in my abilities than I do!" Harry said with a smile.

"Think you can handle it?" Donovan asked.

"This plastic stuff is new to me, but I've handled explosives before. I'll manage. Do you see any other concerns in the plan?"

"Nope. I'll have one of my guys deliver the truck though. I trust them. I'll let Eden know. You just tell him when you need it. Which will be soon I suspect. My sources have the krauts here day after tomorrow."

"I plan on the inspection tomorrow. It shouldn't take long. I'll come back to get Churchill and then head for Scotland. Can you make sure the driver brings some extra petrol cans?"

"He'll have them. You gonna make the run alone then?"

"Just me, Churchill and the driver." Harry said.

"Probably best. The fewer the better." Donovan replied. He then sat upright, staring across the street.

"You see that fellow across the way in the blue navy coat, Harry?"

Harry trained his eyes across the street and immediately spotted the man. He had a navy watch cap on and his hands cupped to his mouth like he was warming them. Harry couldn't see his face. The man was watching them, but when he saw them both looking in his direction he began to walk north around the sandbag barricade in front of the treasury building.

"He seems a bit too interested in us Harry. I saw him earlier when he crossed the park down by those lovebirds. What say we flush him out and see what he's up to?" Donovan said as he stood.

"Alright. I'll head south and you go north. We'll see which one he follows." Harry said as he rose from the bench and started in the direction of the young couples. Out of the corner of his eye he watched the man. The man stopped and retraced his steps in front of the treasury. He seemed to be interested in Harry, but he noticed the man glance around and follow Donovan with his gaze.

The man satisfied they were splitting up, continued on the far side of the street in parallel to Harry's movements. Harry darted across Birdcage Walk and continued down Old Q Street. Just before he reached Dart he came to a pile of rubble. He stepped behind the rubble and looked out to see if the man followed. A minute later the man appeared at the head of Old Q Street. He stopped and surveyed the surroundings then followed in Harry's direction.

When the man passed the rubble, Harry jumped out and wrapped his arms around the stranger's neck. The man grabbed at Harry's arms. When he knew he couldn't break his grip he ran backwards, ramming Harry against the wall. Harry's grip loosened as he grunted from the pain but he didn't let go. "Bloody hell!" the man croaked and tried to flip Harry over his back but Harry swung sideways and threw him off balance.

Both Harry and the man fell to the street. Harry landed on his left elbow and with the excruciating pain; he had to let go of his grip on the man's neck. Freed, the man tried to stand but Harry kicked him in the knee and the man crumpled to the ground again. As Harry scrambled to his feet, holding the wounded arm, the man rolled over and crawled to a sitting position against the wall.

"Jesus, Mr. Lloyd! " he coughed, both hands rubbing his neck, "Is this any way to treat a friend?"

"George old friend. What brings you to this neighborhood?" Harry asked as he recognized George, Mosely's man.

Just then Donovan came running up with a pistol in his hand.

Harry looked at the gun then at Donovan.

George struggled to his feet. He glanced at Harry, then Donovan. Seeing the gun, his shoulders slumped.

Nodding at Donovan, George said to Harry "I suppose if I told you I just happened to be visiting friends in the neighborhood, you wouldn't believe it."

"No George, I wouldn't." Harry said.

"You two know each other?" Donovan asked arching his eyebrows.

"Oh, yes. George and I have a mutual friend, Lord Mosely. The leader of the BFU." Harry said looking at George.

"The British Fascist Union? Well now, that is interesting!" Donovan said.

"Why don't you open your coat George and let's see if you are hiding anything from us." Donovan said as he flicked the gun.

George did as he was asked. He had an American Colt .45 in his waistband that Harry promptly relieved him of.

"Rather an odd weapon for an Englishman, isn't it, Bill?" Harry asked as he displayed the gun in front of Donovan.

"Not so strange nowadays. You Brits have gotten a ton of those from us since the war started. I'm sure some have made their way to the black market."

Harry turned back to George.

"Now George, please explain how you happened to be here." Harry said as he put the heavy gun into his coat pocket. He quickly retrieved it when he suddenly thought of the explosives and the small arsenal he now carried.

"Mr. Mosely wanted to know what you were up to. He thinks you're playing some kind of game. You upset him last night by the way." George said as he buttoned his coat back up.

"I meant to upset him. You do know your boss is crazy don't you?" Harry asked.

"He's a bit daft, that's for sure. But he pays well. He doesn't pay well enough for me to get shot though." George said nodding at the gun in Donovan's hand.

"What exactly were you to find out?" Donovan asked.

"Nothing in particular. Just whom Mr. Lloyd met, what he did, where he went. That sort of thing."

"Tell us some more about Mr. Mosely's friends." Donovan said.

"Mostly members of the BFU. Some are members of parliament. In fact more have joined since the armistice was signed. There is also a German fellow who visits quite a bit. I think he is the real boss, not Mr. Mosely."

"How much do know about the BFU George?" Harry asked.

"Not much. I don't attend the meetings. I mean I go there, but I stand outside to make sure only members attend. They do a lot of the crazy 'Heil Hitler' stuff and bitch about the Jews. But I think they have big plans when the Germans arrive. They get together a lot more now and Mr. Mosely has been getting more visitors."

"Do you know the name of this German?" Donovan asked.

"No. I don't think anyone has ever addressed him by name. But he is a young fellow. Real cocky type." George said.

"Well George, since you have been so honest, I'm going to give you a choice. You know I work for the government don't you?" Harry asked.

"Yes. Mr. Mosely told me you were some sort of diplomat but you're now working for MI5. I figure that to be true, 'cause no diplomat could've got the drop on me like you did!" George said instinctively reaching for his throat.

Donovan and Harry exchanged quick glances.

"Okay George, your choice. We have you arrested for accosting a government official…"

George looked as if he were going to interrupt then closed his mouth. Harry continued: "Mr. Donovan will attest to the fact you attacked me."

George looked from Donovan to Harry and then nodded his head. He understood the setup.

"If we arrest you, your boss will know you failed. And my guess is he isn't a man to tolerate failure. The other choice is we let you go. You return to your boss and report on what a dull day I've had. You don't mention I was at Whitehall or that I met with this gentleman. Got it?"

"You spent the whole day at home with that women you live with. Maybe went for a walk alone?" George asked. Understanding perfectly well

Harry nodded his head. "The woman is my aunt and yes, you seem to understand. Now how do we know you won't change stories when you get back?"

"You don't. You just have to understand, Mr. Mosely is my only source of income but going to jail isn't one of my favorite ideas. I have a phobia about queers."

"All right run along then. If either of us gets wind of this conversation, from anyone, George, I'll see to it that you go to prison wearing a pink jump suit with a target on your ass. Got it?"

George visibly shuddered. "Not a word. This never happened, Mr. Lloyd." George shook his head.

Donovan put the gun back into his pocket and he and Harry headed back towards Whitehall. George turned and went in the opposite direction.

"We have a leak somewhere, Bill. No one knew of my reassignment to MI5 but Eden and Churchill." Harry said when they back on the street.

"And the MI5 chief who signed your papers." Donovan added.

"Since you are so chummy with the intelligence folks, can you dig around and see what you can find out?" Harry asked.

"I'll head over there now. I'll also do some digging on this German fellow he mentioned. You take care Harry. You seem to be able to handle yourself pretty well, but there are a lot of people who can do it better. Not all of them are your friends. Let Eden know when you need the truck. I'll see that it gets there." Donovan said as he started across the street.

Harry watched him for a moment then headed for the tube station. Instead of heading back to the flat, Harry took the tube to Wapping Street. The effects of the German bombs became more apparent as he neared the East Side. Hundreds of blank-faced people milled about in the underground. People huddled around makeshift beds and a few open fires.

"Poor bastards." He thought, the anger beginning to rise. Thousands had lost their homes during the German Blitz. There were hundreds of shelters setup through out the city but they couldn't handle all the people who had nowhere to go. Many wound up in the underground tunnels of the tube system.

He exited the underground at Wapping and wandered out onto the street. The devastation was tremendous. Whole blocks of homes, offices and warehouses were nothing but piles of rubble. Fire and street cleaning brigades worked around the clock trying to clear debris. The armistice had brought relief from the bombing and no fires were evident except for a few plumes of smoke wafting up from a couple of heaps of masonry and wood. A home guard official stood near one of the piles. Harry approached him and showed him his MI5 badge.

"I'm Colonel Lloyd. I need to have a closer look at the damage here. Is it safe?" Harry asked.

"Never safe. Could be unexploded bombs in there. That's why I'm here. To make sure no one goes poking around and gets hurt." The elderly official said, puffing his chest out with pride and eyeing Harry suspiciously.

"And I appreciate that, er, Sergeant?" Harry said, as he looked for insignia on the man's uniform.

Indignant, the man replied, "Sergeant *Major,* sir!"

"Yes, well sergeant major, I'm going over there and take a closer look. Official business." Harry said and proceeded to walk around the old man towards the pile.

"If you blows yourself up, don't blame me!" the man yelled after him.

Harry smiled as he reached into his coat pocket and pulled out a piece of the putty about the size of an American dime. He took a fuse out of the other pocket, rolled the putty into a ball and stuck the fuse in it. He moved to the side of the pile, away from the guard's view and knelt down. He placed the bomb under a beam and a small section of wall that stuck out from the pile, turned the fuse, straightened and walked back to the guard.

"Tell me sergeant major," Harry said as he grabbed the old man's arm and gently pulled him along further out into the street. "How many buildings were destroyed here?"

"Don't really know." The man said scratching the stubble on his chin and eyeing the block up and down as if counting the buildings. He suddenly looked at Harry and said, "You gents bloody well ought to know! Your bloody intelligence aren't you?"

Harry was about reply when a muffled explosion came from the pile. Except for flying dust, very little evidence of an explosion could be seen.

"What in bloody hell was that!" the old man yelled as he put his hand over his helmet as if he thought it was going to blow off. He stuffed a whistle in his mouth with his other hand and began to blow the shrill whistle in every direction.

"You best move out of here mister! I believe we have a live bomb in there! It could be just a start of a major blow!" He said grabbing Harry by the arm and pulling him down the street away from the pile.

Harry didn't protest. He had seen enough. He removed the man's hand from his arm and said, "You're right sergeant major. I don't feel too safe here. I'll be on my way!"

Chuckling to himself, he hurried in the direction of the tube he had exited a short time ago. As he entered the tube, he could hear the sound of a fire engine siren wailing in the distance.

"I guess their day will be a bit more lively!" he said to himself as he settled on the train.

#

When George arrived back at Mosely's home, he went straight to the study to report the story as Lloyd had dictated. He found Mosely having a drink with the German.

"Ah, George! What do you have to report on our mysterious Mr. Lloyd?" Mosely greeted him.

George looked at the German and back at Mosely with a questioning look.

"Don't worry George, General Schellenberg is an esteemed member of the German SS organization. He probably already knows what you're going to say." Mosely said as he winked at the General.

"You can say what you have to say in front of him.

George saw the German's head jerk towards Mosely at the mention of his name. The look told George he was not pleased.

"Mr. Lloyd has spent the day at his home with the woman. I was able to determine the woman is his Aunt." George reported.

"That's it? No visitors? He went nowhere?" Mosely replied, sounding surprised and angered by the news.

"No one came and he never left." George affirmed.

"And you stayed at your post all day? You didn't find some pub to perhaps eat or quench your thirst?" Mosely asked suspiciously.

"No sir. I brought a thermos of coffee and a sandwich with me. I never left."

"All right. Thank you George. Take a break and return this evening. I want to know if he gets any visitors in the night." Mosely said as he ushered George out the door, closing it after George was deposited in the hall.

George could hear the German's voice rumbling through the closed door. He had been right. The German was not pleased. Frowning, his mind clouding with thoughts, George headed to the kitchen to make and eat the fictitious sandwich he had said he had.

As he ate, George heard the German leave. Mosely entered the kitchen leaned against the doorjamb and watched George.

"Well, George. Your plans have changed. The General was impressed with your surveillance of Mr. Lloyd. He has asked that you meet him tonight at Trafalgar Square at eight o'clock. I suggest you be prompt." Mosely said as he turned and left the kitchen.

George finished his sandwich and took a bottle of ale from the icebox. He sat at the table and drank it slowly. "Might suspicious, that." George thought, "There could be only one reason the German would want to see me and I don't believe it is at all good."

He pondered the situation for a moment, his brow furrowed and his mouth locked in a half-bite.

"George, you just can't seem to keep a job." He said to himself. "Perhaps mother was right: you *are* just plain worthless."

He took another drink.

CHAPTER 10

Harry sat at the dining table; the gun he had taken from George lay in front of him. The more he thought it over the more he felt he might need it. He had decided he would strip it down and clean it while he waited for Eden.

Thankfully, Agnes had gone to her room early. He didn't want to have to explain the gun. She had taken to sleeping draughts since the blitz, and Harry knew he would be undisturbed. The gun seemed to be in good order and the clip was full. He leaned forward towards the light. The sun had set a half an hour ago and he worked under the glow of a small desk lamp.

He heard a loud pounding at the front door. He stood and walked down the hall to the entrance. The entranceway was dark and as he reached to turn on the entrance light, he thought better of it. Eden wasn't one to pound on a door. Whoever it was meant to get his attention. He stepped to the side of the door, turned the handle and swung it open. No bullets flew into the open doorway and he felt a little foolish. He stuck his head around to peer out the entrance and was surprised to see George standing there.

"A bit cautious Mr. Lloyd?" he asked with a dumb grin on his face.

"Let's just say I'm playing it safe." Harry said as he stepped into the doorway. "What are you doing here? Your boss wants another chat?" Harry asked.

"No. Could I please step inside? I think I need to begin to play it safe myself." George begged as he glanced around behind him.

Harry sensed fear and urgency in George's voice. He looked past George to see if anyone else may be lurking in the shadows. Seeing no one, he stepped back and waved George in. George stepped into the entranceway. Harry shut the door and walked past George down to the kitchen entrance.

"Come on George. We can talk in here." He said stepping into the kitchen. George followed.

"Have a seat." Harry said. George pulled out one of the chairs around the table and sat. He eyed the gun on the table.

"Breaking it or fixing it?" George asked, nodding towards the table.

"Cleaning it." Harry said as he sat. "What brings you here? You seem a bit anxious."

"Let's just say my employer has decided to pinch a few pennies, mainly by getting rid of the hired help." George said looking down at his big hands.

"Mosely dismissed you? Because of what happened today?" Harry asked a little surprised.

George looked up and shook his head.

"Not what happened between us. As you had so persuasively suggested, I told him you hadn't left the house all day." George replied with a wry grin.

"He didn't seem to believe me, but I don't think that had much to do with what happened. The German fellow was there when I got back. Mosely let slip his name in front of me. When I left the room, I heard the German guy yelling at Mosely. After the German left, Mosely said I was to meet the German down at Trafalgar tonight, about now as a matter of fact." George said as he looked to the clock on the wall above the stove.

"There is only one reason I can think of that the German would want to see me. I think he means to kill me because I now know who he is." George explained, as he eyed Harry wondering if he believed him.

Harry watched the other man for a moment, decided he was telling the truth and said: "Why'd you come here? I'm certainly not hiring!"

"I know that. I didn't come looking for a job. I don't want money either. I thought maybe, in exchange for the German's name, you could get me out of the country. You know, pull a few strings at the office?" George said giving a weak imitation of a grin.

"I don't know beans about you, Mr. Lloyd," He continued, "But I think you're intelligent and honest man. I also think you are a fair man. Hell, you could have had me by me balls today, but you let me go. Not many men in your position would have."

Before Harry could respond, they were interrupted by another knock at the door.

"Eden." Harry thought.

"Excuse me a minute George. Don't run off. If this is who I think it is, we might be able to work something out." Harry said as he stood.

As he started from the kitchen, he had another thought and turned back to the table and picked up the gun.

George looked from the gun to Harry.

"Don't trust me, eh?" He said nodding at the gun.

"Just removing the temptation." Harry said and left to answer the door.

Harry peeked out the small window next to the door this time. It was Eden, and he had brought Donovan with him. Harry opened the door and greeted them. Both visitors looked at the gun and then to Harry.

"I'll explain in a minute." Harry said as he turned and led them to the kitchen.

As they entered the kitchen, both of the new visitors spotted George. George grinned and nodded his recognition to Donovan.

Eden and Donovan looked from George to Harry with perplexed expressions.

"Anthony, I'd like you to meet, George. George, Anthony Eden, the British Foreign Secretary. You have already met my other guest but you weren't formally introduced. This is Mr. Donovan. An American." Harry said as way of introduction.

George stood awkwardly and stuck his hand out. Donovan shook it but Eden ignored him and turned to Harry.

"What is this? Isn't he the fellow Bill told me about? The man who was tailing you today?" He said with a combination of surprise and anger in his voice.

"Yes. Relax, Anthony." Harry replied as he put his hand on Eden's arm in reassurance.

"I believe George here is going to become an ally. He has some information I feel you'll find interesting. He knows the name of the German fellow." Harry said as he motioned for the two newcomers to sit.

"The German who is pulling the strings for Mosely?" Donovan asked incredulously as he looked at George. He took off his coat, draped it over a chair and sat.

"Yes. Tell them what you told me George." Harry answered as he sat back into the chair he had vacated. He placed the gun back on the table in front of him.

George repeated the account of his meeting with Mosely.

Eden, who had remained standing, now removed his coat and sat.

"He doesn't know anything does he Harry?" Eden asked.

"About us? No. He only wishes safe passage to any continent that doesn't have Germans on it. Isn't that right George?" Harry replied as he looked to George.

"That's right. But if I'm about to hear more shit that can get my ass shot off, I'll leave and find some other way!" George said as he held his hands up in front of him as if warding off evil.

"Nobody is going to shoot you, George. At least not yet. What was the name you heard by the way?" Donovan asked.

George looked around the table. He felt like a trapped animal. Mosely and his gang were scary but something about a foreign minister, a diplomat turned intelligence officer and an unknown American meeting together at night was scarier.

He had escaped the criminal gangs of the eastside and all the inherent dangers to find a nice cushy job as a bodyguard for a rich former Member of Parliament. He even had time to invest in his favorite hobby: reading. He had thought life was good. Until today that is.

He placed his hands, palms up, before him and said, "Look, the name means nothing to me. I only thought Mr. Lloyd would want it because of the questions he asked me earlier. I'm a nobody who came from nowhere. I don't want any trouble."

"Like it or not. You have found yourself in the middle of a lot of trouble. Tell us the name and we'll figure out what we'll do with you later." Eden said sternly, eyes narrowed.

George looked at Harry beseechingly.

"George, have you ever served in the military?" Harry asked suddenly.

George was surprised by the question and his expression showed it. Eden and Donovan were also taken aback by the question and they both looked to Harry questioningly.

"No. I was too young for the last war and I, well, sort of forgot to register for this one." George said glancing at Eden then looking back to Harry.

Eden snorted and said "Very good young men have given their life for their country and you have been living the good life, dodging your responsibilities!" Nodding at the gun on the table, he continued, "If that gun were loaded. I'd shoot you right now!" He glared at George, visibly shaking with anger.

George cringed and looked down at his hands.

Donovan, catching on to Harry's line of thinking, stepped in.

"George, if given the chance, would you enlist?"

George looked up questioningly. "If I set foot in a recruitment center, I'd be arrested on the spot!" he said, aghast at the very idea.

Harry shook his head and leaned forward, placing his arms crosswise onto the table.

"Not necessarily. Look, I have a mission I need to accomplish. You need to escape some surly Nazi bunch. You have a name His Majesty's Government is very eager to have. I think we can work an arrangement where everyone is happy. Well at least satisfied. Anthony?" Harry said looking at Eden.

Eden scowled at Harry, and looked to Donovan who nodded his head.

"You trust this man that much?" Eden asked Harry. His expression was one of shock.

Harry nodded.

"I think I do trust him." Harry said as he looked to George. Then turning back to Eden, "We can't let him go for fear he may talk. We can't arrest him for the same reason and I won't have him murdered." Harry said, thinking of the men who had worked on the Enigma.

Eden pondered this for a moment and then sighed as he nodded his head.

"If he agrees to enlist and serve his full time, causing no trouble, I think I can arrange it so he doesn't go to jail." Eden said flatly, looking at George.

"What do you think?' Harry asked turning to George.

"How long I gotta serve?" George asked. Then waved his hand in dismissal at Eden who appeared to be getting ready for another outburst.

"Oh forget it. I don't have much choice do I? Where do I sign?" George said, shoulders slumped in resignation.

Donavan laughed, leaned over and slapped George on the back. "You'll do fine! Besides the British army will probably go out of existence once the Germans get here."

Eden glowered at Donovan.

George brightened for a moment then frowned. "Seems to me I'm back in the same predicament I started from!" he cried.

Eden folded his arms across his chest and triumphantly gloated, "And justice shall prevail!"

Harry reached over and put his hand on Eden's arm and shook his head. He turned to George.

"You are now part of His Majesty's Royal Army. We'll get to the paperwork later. As of now you are assigned to my mission and me. By this time tomorrow you'll be far from London lad."

"Now just a minute Harry, you don't have the authority to do that! You can't just arbitrarily pick and choose who is or is not qualified for military service like that! There are procedures, man! I—"

Harry, resuming the role of mission leader, turned to Eden.

"Anthony, I have a mission to accomplish. You yourself said it was up to me how I accomplish it. I can't do it alone and I trust George. Expediency is called for here. I'm just doing what is expedient. As I explained earlier, we can't just let George go." Harry's voice left no room for argument.

Eden looked around the table again, thinking. Finally he turned to George and asked resignedly, "What are your measurements? I'll need to get a uniform over here before morning."

Harry smiled at Eden and turned back to George, "What is the name you overheard?"

"Schellenberg. General Schellenberg." George replied, resigned to the fact he was in it now, for better or worse.

"General Walther Schellenberg! That's the bastard that set your MI6 agents and up in Holland!" Donovan cried.

"At Venlo?" Eden queried.

"Yes, Captain Best and Major Stevens. They are in some German concentration camp now. What the hell is he doing here?"

"No doubt he is the Nazi point man." Harry said. "What I want to know is what is his interest in me?" He looked at George.

"I don't know! I don't even know if he knew Mosely was having me follow you." George said, alarmed at the look on the faces staring at him.

"He must know I have never contacted the Germans. He'll know my sympathizer cover is a sham." Harry said, somewhat alarmed.

"Not necessarily, Harry. The Germans have a turf war going on in intelligence. The Abwehr - German army intelligence branch, and the SD—Himmler's SS intelligence branch, are forever at odds over who does what. Since Schellenberg is SD, it's possible he thinks you are an Abwehr agent. He may be trying to determine that. That's why he is using Mosely." Donovan interjected.

"By the way MI5 found their leak. They have had their eye on her for a while now. In fact she lives not to far from here. Her name is Lily Sergeyev. She worked in the ministry offices and uses the code name Treasure. They picked her up this afternoon after I mentioned our run-in with George here. She didn't resist at all and was quite talkative. She saw Anthony's memo to MI5 about your transfer and passed it on to a contact in Mosely's gang. They don't know who the contact was though. He had a code name too." Donovan added.

"Then I have no choice but to make my move tomorrow. George what I am about to tell you *WILL* get you killed if it leaks." Harry looked at George and told him his mission, referring to the Enigma only as 'the package', and his plan to accomplish it. George's jaw dropped at the mention of Churchill, but he listened intently.

"Tomorrow you will be my lorry driver. We'll go over the details of exactly what I want you to do later. Understand?" Harry concluded.

"I got it." George nodded. He liked the plan. He especially liked the part about going to Ireland. Once he made it there, it was going to be bye-bye army. Somehow he knew Harry understood this too.

"Let me make that call about George's uniform. I will really need your measurements this time, George." Eden said as he stood. George told him.

Harry told him where the telephone was. "You better make him a sergeant." He said after Eden. Eden stopped and turned around ready to reply, thought better of it and turned back, grunting in reply.

Both Harry and Donovan grinned at George. Smiling, George rolled his eyes and shook his head.

They continued to discuss the plans until after midnight. It was decided that George, with Donovan's assistance, would pick up the lorry at the motor pool at nine in the morning. Returning to pick up Harry, they would leave for Bletchley by ten. Donovan would make sure light weapons were hidden on the lorry, in case they were needed, as well as extra petrol cans. Harry added that perhaps a change of clothes would be needed also. To save time, Churchill would be driven to Bletchley in a curtained vehicle and the lorry would rendezvous with him after getting the Enigma and plans.

A few minutes after Eden and Donovan left to update Churchill, an Army corporal delivered George's uniform complete with polished shoes.

George held it as if it were garbage needing to be thrown out. Harry chuckled to himself as he took George upstairs and showed George to the spare bedroom.

"Make sure you put it on right. Let me have a look at you before we leave in the morning." Harry said as he nodded at the uniform.

"Goodnight George. Oh, by the way what is your last name? I can't be calling you Sergeant George now can I?" Harry asked as he turned to leave.

"It's Hayes. George Hayes." George replied, hanging the uniform on the closet door and placing the shoes next to the bed.

Harry nodded, "Goodnight then, Sergeant Hayes." He said as he walked from the room. He returned downstairs to the kitchen and began to re-assemble the gun. He had a gnawing suspicion he may need it.

CHAPTER 11

The man in the black trench coat walked nervously back and forth in front of the tube station at Trafalgar. He had been given the description of a man that would be arriving from Hampstead around eight o'clock. He had been watching since half-past seven. He rolled the glove back on his left hand and peered at this watch again. It read nine-twenty. The man obviously wasn't going to show. He waited for the next train and boarded it. He would report to his master then set off on another night of entertainment. Wartime or not, if you had the money and knew where to look, London still had a lot to offer a man with certain tastes.

"He never showed?" Schellenberg spat. He and the man who had been watching for George at Trafalgar, stood in an anteroom of the house a BFU member had given Schellenberg.

"Wait here. I may have more work for you." Schellenberg ordered as he left the room. The man, seeing his night of fun disappear, sat dejectedly in the only chair in the room.

Schellenberg entered the large library where the rich and powerful English guests he was entertaining waited.

Among the guests were John Amery, son of Leopold Stennet Amery, Great Britain's former Minister for India, and a member of Churchill's wartime cabinet. John Amery was vehemently anti-Communist and he greatly admired the order and discipline of fascist Germany. His father knew nothing of his associations and John preferred it that way, at least until the Nazis had officially taken over the British government. He would then show his father and his stuffy friends what governing was all about.

Schellenberg approached Amery.

"Mosely's man never showed. Mosely phoned when the man left so I have to assume he figured out what was going to happen and has gone underground." He whispered to Amery as he took him aside.

"That leaves you in a bit of pickle then doesn't it?" Amery said with an amused smile on his face.

"He knows who you are. If he tells the wrong people before your friends arrive, the security services might take matters into their own hands. Technically you are an enemy spy."

Amery despised the arrogant gaunt faced Schellenberg and loved any opportunity to make him feel uncomfortable.

"Not to mention your own neck. I don't think they would take too kindly to having a traitor in their midst either." Schellenberg hissed with a look of disgust at Amery. "We need to find him. Or I should say, you need to find him. In the meantime, I'll radio Berlin. Himmler must send his advance party as soon as possible. I think your government is using this lull to bury secrets that may prove to be valuable to our people. Find out from Mosely where the man usually goes, who is friends are, anything that will help locate him." Schellenberg said.

Amery's bemused look turned deadly as he replied, "I'll call Mosely and afterwards I'll also send some friends of mine around to pay him a visit. The old fool has lost his usefulness. Those still loyal to him in the BFU will follow my directions if he is removed."

Schellenberg nodded in agreement.

"I have no further use for him. Don't make it look obvious. We don't need the police involved. I'm sure a man of his drinking habits could feasibly have an accident." Schellenberg said, straightening and smiling at one of his guests who was eyeing them suspiciously.

"I'll leave it up to you. Now go call Mosely and your friends. My guests here are getting suspicious. I don't want them asking questions. If

they smell danger they'll pull their support. We can't have that this close
to the occupation." Schellenberg said as he started towards one of the
guests, smiling.

Amery followed. When Schellenberg stopped to chat with the guest
he continued on towards the door. He stopped suddenly when he heard
Schellenberg call his name.

Schellenberg approached Amery and whispered, "Include our Mr.
Lloyd in your plans for this evening. I don't know what he is up to but
Mosely suspects him of something. I can't afford to be surprised. You
can use Mr. O'Malley. I left him in the room across the hall. He's simple
but he does good work." Dismissing Avery, he then turned and walked
over to a group of guests.

Amery left the library and entered the anteroom. O'Malley jumped up
from where he had been sitting. He held his rumpled hat in his hands.

"Mr. O'Malley? Mr. Schellenberg said you might be able to assist me."
Amery smiled at the man.

#

Kevin O' Malley, whose father had been murdered in the 1916 Easter
uprising in Ireland, hated the British. He had come to London looking
for a way to get even. He had found sympathetic friends, all from
Ireland, and together they had committed small but satisfying terrorist
acts for the past two years. About a year ago a man dressed like a tourist
with a heavy German accent had approached him. The man had offered
a great deal of money to Kevin and his friends if they would do some
work for him. The work had turned out to be pretty boring stuff: find-
ing addresses of parliament members who had a dolly on the side, following politicians around and reporting anything they did which may
prove embarrassing. There were quite a few powerful people in government who had skeletons in their closets and he and his friends had been

able to accumulate a lot of money. Money they used to purchase explosives and weapons.

He now carried some of those items as he and two of his friends made their way to a Hampstead address of a Mr. Lloyd. It was nearly half-past midnight, O'Malley noticed as he glanced at his watch. Amery had said Schellenberg wanted Mr. Lloyd 'removed from the stage'.

O'Malley and his gang were not intellectuals. They approached a job with a simple determination. Their plan was to bomb the house and shoot anyone who tried to escape. O'Malley figure it would take twenty minutes tops. On foot, they would be scattered in all directions before any police showed.

The three assassins approached the house from across the street near the cemetery. O' Malley looked up and down the deserted street then pulled a stick of dynamite from the bag he carried. His accomplices spread out behind the cemetery wall covering the front exit to the house with American-made Thompson machine guns. O'Malley nodded to each man then lit the dynamite and hurled it at the window in the front of the house.

Harry heard the glass break as he finished wiping the gun. He had no time to register its meaning before a tremendous explosion rocked the house. Instinct made him dive under the kitchen table as the wall separating the front room from the kitchen came hurtling towards him in a hundred pieces.

Partially deaf, his ears ringing from the blast, Harry crawled out from under the table. Pieces of plaster and wood were strewn all about. The portrait of his father that had adorned the front room wall lay shattered at his feet. He coughed and squinted his eyes. The smoke and dust from the explosion limited his vision and made breathing difficult. Surprisingly the lamp was still glowing under the chair where it had fallen. He turned towards the doorway as he heard coughing and gagging coming from the direction of the staircase in the hall.

George's mass filled the doorway.

"What the hell happened? The Germans begin bombing us again?" George asked as he staggered over the debris into the kitchen. He helped Harry to his feet and retrieved the lamp.

Harry looked at the destruction around him. When he turned to where the wall had been, he suddenly screamed, "Oh my God! Agnes! Give me a hand George!"

Harry fell to his hands and knees as he climbed over the rubble towards the front room. George's eyes followed Harry. When he held the lamp up and peered into the front room, he saw that the upper floor had crashed down into the front room. There was a crumpled bed in the middle of what looked like a chest of drawers and broken glass from a mirror. A body appeared to be lying on the bed. He put the lamp onto the rubble-strewn table and scrambled after Harry.

When Harry reached the bed, he pulled a broken drawer from the body of Agnes. As he struggled to lift her, he saw a shard of glass had cut cleanly through her neck. Blood, thick with dust, stained the sheets.

Harry cried a wail of anguish and lowered Agnes back onto the bed. He swung around to George with murder in his eyes.

"Who the hell did this? Why?" he shouted then suddenly, eyes narrowed, he turned and grabbed George.

"Mosely followed you! This was meant for you, you bastard!" He spat at George.

George grabbed Harry's wrists and pulled them from his collar.

"This isn't Mosely's style." George said calmly, holding Harry's arms in his massive hands.

"Harry, this was meant for you!"

Harry stared at George with pure hatred, and then as he began to gain control, his contorted face slowly relaxed. George released his grip and Harry ran his hand nervously through his hair as he turned and looked at Agnes' body. He looked back to George then stumbled back to the kitchen. He grabbed the lamp as he pushed the table away from him. He fell to his knees and dug into the rubble. After a brief moment, he stood with the gun in his hand.

"You have any more bullets for this?" He said looking at George.

George climbed through the debris and stood next to Harry. "Upstairs. In my coat. I'll get them." He said as he scrambled back up the unsteady stairs. He returned in a moment carrying the British Army uniform, shoes and all. He handed Harry two full clips of bullets.

Harry's training took over and he was considerably calmer now. He loaded the clip into the gun and pocketed the extra clips.

He looked up suddenly.

"Wait here a moment George. There is something I can't leave behind." He said as he headed for the stairs.

Harry returned a short time later with a bag.

"Let's get out of here. I don't want to get detained by any police. He said as he took one last look into the front room and headed for the hallway. The door had been blown off its hinges and the window near the door was strewn all around in silvery pieces. As he approached the hole where the door had been, he tripped on a piece of wood and stumbled to his knees. At that moment a hail of bullets flew above his head, plastering the cracked ceiling above him and the wall to his right. Pulling himself up into a crouch, he turned to see if George had been hit. He saw George lying face down on the floor.

"George! Are you hit?" he yelled.

George moved, and then lifted his head. His head and face was covered in blood. Harry's first thought was that George had been shot in the face.

George waved his hand at Harry and replied, "I'm fine. Got some pieces of glass in my hands and face when I dived to the floor, but I'll live. What the hell is going on Harry? You piss off a neighbor or something?"

George crawled to the doorway next to Harry.

"I don't know. I didn't think anyone knew about us. We've got to get out of here and try to grab the bastard!" Harry said as he tried to see through the smoke and dust to the street outside.

"Killing you, Harry. Not us. You." George said patting Harry on the shoulder.

They both turned as a loud crackling sound came from the front room on their left. Flames had begun to appear from beneath the rubble.

"I'm going to crawl over to those shrubs on my right." Harry said, nodding to the small shrubs that lined the front of the house.

"What the hell are you going to do when you get there? He seems to have the whole front covered." George asked.

"I'm going to try to see who is shooting at us. You try to get him to fire again. When I see the fire from his gun, I'll shoot at it." Harry answered, pointing in the direction of the street.

Harry grabbed his bag, crawled over the threshold and rolled under the shrub. When he was in position to look out at the street he turned and waved to George. The fire in the house was slowly lighting the street, but Harry couldn't see anybody.

George looked around for something to get the gunman's attention. He saw a two-foot piece of plaster wall lying near the front room entrance. He crawled over and grabbed it. He held the plaster above his head with one hand as he crawled back to the doorway. As he neared the door, shots rang out and the plaster disintegrated in his hand. The deep rumble of the unseen gunman's weapon was followed by a sharper crack from Harry's pistol. A cry was heard then two unintelligible voices yelled from somewhere outside. A burst of automatic weapon fire tore into the doorway for a second and another crack from Harry's pistol was heard, followed by a scream. George scrambled out to the bush near Harry.

"Sounds like you got 'em. Nice shooting. Learn that in diplomatic school, Harry?" He asked as he neared Harry.

Harry ignored him. "They're by the cemetery. The two I hit stepped out from behind the trees. I think there is a third person out there. I thought I heard two voices after I shot the first gunmen." He said leaning to his right trying to see across the street.

Near the cemetery wall, he saw a flare of a match and a bright light. He grabbed the bag in one hand and George with the other and yelled, "Get moving, I think he just lit a fuse!"

He and George scrambled up from behind the bush and ran, crouching, towards the street. A second later, the explosion blew them both out onto the pavement.

Harry hit hands first and flipped head over heels, losing the gun and the bag. George, who had landed and tumbled up on his knees, dove at the pistol lying in the street. He looked up and fired at a target running away from them. The man's hands flew up and a bag he was carrying flipped into the air.

Both men scrambled to their feet and ran towards the now prone man.

Harry rolled him over and was glad to see he was still alive. Blood dribbled from Kevin O'Malley's mouth as he tried to say something. Harry knelt down trying to hear.

"Ireland forever! You bastard!" O'Malley mumbled.

"What the hell are you taking about, man?" Harry cried as he shook the dying man.

"You tried to kill me as some sort of revenge for Ireland? Why?" He yelled into the man's face.

"Nazis'll finish you, just wait!" O'Malley whispered.

O'Malley could feel the life draining from his body. He felt no pain. Only a cold numbness. He closed his eyes and waited for the devil to claim his soul.

"Who hired you? Who put you up to this?" Harry yelled at the man's face.

"Easy, Harry. The man's dying. You won't get anymore from him." George said as he put his hand on Harry's shoulder.

Harry looked up at George and said, "He said something about Ireland and that the Nazis will finish it. What the hell does that mean?"

"I don't know. Doesn't make much sense. The Irish part I mean. Everyone knows the German's are coming so that's not a surprise. What bothers me is why you? Why was he sent after you?" George asked.

Harry looked down at the man, thought of Agnes and pushed the man away in disgust and stood up.

Kevin O'Malley, small time Irish avenger, coughed up blood, tried to suck in one last breath, failed, and died.

Suddenly a hail of bullets tore up the pavement all around them. They both dove to the curb. George looked up and saw one of the gunmen Harry had shot was on his knees with an American Thompson machine gun pointed in their direction. He aimed and fired the pistol. The gun flew from the man's hand and skittered onto the street.

George followed his shot on a dead run, getting to the gunmen ahead of Harry.

The man lay on the grass near the curb moaning. George's bullet had caught him in his bicep and George saw blood pouring from a wound on the man's head that was deep enough to show bone.

"All right lad. What the hell is going on here?" He said, reaching down and lifting the man up by his shattered arm. The man screamed in pain, but staggered to his feet.

Harry ran up as the man stood and grabbed him by his collar.

"Who the hell are you people? What do want with me?" He yelled into the man's bloodied face.

The man staggered and his legs gave out. George held him up.

"Answer the man or I'll start twisting this arm bit by bit until it comes off." George said into the man's ear as he shook the mangled arm.

The man's head lolled back and forth for a moment then his eyes focused on Harry. "It was O'Malley's idea." He said through tight blood-drained lips."

"Who the hell is O'Malley?" Harry yelled.

The man closed his eyes and moaned. George squeezed his arm. His eyes shot open and he screamed. "The man you shot down the road!" he cried. "He was hired by some bigshot's kid to kill Lloyd!"

Harry looked at George in puzzlement. George squeezed again.

"Christ! Stop it! I'll talk! I'll talk! Just quit squeezing my arm!" the man screamed.

Harry nodded at George and George lowered the man to the pavement and leaned down beside him.

"Who was O'Malley and which bigshot?" George asked into the man's ear.

"O'Malley...was from Ireland. His father...His father was killed in '16. He has been doing some jobs for this German guy on and off for the...last year. Mainly spying on bigwigs, but we blew some government buildings too." The man moaned.

Harry knelt on one knee in front of their captive. "What was the German's name?"

"I don't know. He always...He always found us. We didn't contact him. The past six...months it's been a different guy. A younger guy. He and the bigshot's kid are friends. I seen 'em together a coupla' times. The kids name is John, John Amery." He choked as he tried to look at Harry, but his eyes wouldn't focus.

Harry was taken back by the mention of Amery. There was only one 'bigshot' named Amery. It had to be Leopold Amery. He had met him when he served in India. That didn't make any sense though. Amery was as loyal as they come. Part of the old school. Why would he be collaborating with the Nazis? The answer was, he wouldn't be. As part of Churchill's cabinet, he'd be on the Nazi blacklist. The kid had to be doing this on his own, without his father's knowledge and certainly without his approval.

"Where do you meet this German?" He asked.

"Usually in Piccadilly, but tonight O'Malley went to his place. Said it was over on Victoria Park. He didn't say an address." The man answered then suddenly convulsed. He jerked loose from George's grip, flipped over onto his stomach, vomited and lay still.

George rolled him over. His eyes were rolled back into his head and he wasn't breathing.

"Won't be saying anymore. Lost too much blood by the looks of it." He said as he stood up. He suddenly became aware that somewhere there was a third gunman. He spun around and walked towards the tree behind them. He found the other gunman sprawled out on the grass, a bullet hole in the forehead. He walked back to Harry who was staring at the dead body at his feet. Harry looked questioningly up as George approached.

"Remembered there was another one them." George said. "You caught him between the eyes."

Suddenly Harry remembered the bag. He turned and saw it lying in the street where he had fallen. He dashed into the street and retrieved it.

"Special toothbrush?" George asked, nodding at the bag as he joined Harry.

"Tools for tomorrows job. Let's get the hell out of here before anyone shows up." He said looking up and down the street.

"Come to think of it, the bobbies are a little slow."

"They've got enough troubles with looting and stuff in the areas that got bombed." George answered," But don't worry they'll show." He said pointing at the house next door to Harry's, where a head was outlined against the sliver of light shining through a pulled back curtain.

Harry followed where he pointed nodded. He turned his gaze to the now burning house, turned, and started off in the direction of the cemetery. Realizing where they were headed, George commented, "As if we haven't seen enough dead people tonight!"

CHAPTER 12

Harry and George made their way to the Foreign Office building and after cleaning up, awaited the arrival of the foreign minister in his office. George's face was swollen and bruised but the bleeding had stopped. Harry had a few cuts on his hands but was otherwise in good shape. Both individual's clothes were torn and covered in dirt and dust.

A haggard looking Eden arrived an hour later.

"Good God Harry! What happened?" He asked, as he surveyed the two.

"We had some visitors. Agnes is dead." Harry replied unemotionally, looking down at a cut on his hand.

"Your Aunt? How? Wait a minute, just start from the beginning, after Donovan and I left. Then I've got some more bad news for you." Eden said as he walked over to the cabinet in the corner of the office.

He took out three glasses and a bottle of bourbon. He filled two of the glasses and handed them to Harry and George. He poured a small amount into his glass and sat on the edge of his desk, giving Harry his full attention.

Harry took a large drink. Looking down into the glass he held on his lap, he told Eden of the attack.

When Harry finished, Eden refilled all three glasses as he thought of what Harry had just said.

Returning to his perch on the edge of his desk, Eden finally asked, "Why would Schellenberg go after you? Your mission is only known by the three of us in this room and Winston of course."

"I've asked myself that question a hundred times in the past three hours. I can only come up with one link between us and that is Mosely. He couldn't have known George came to me, so that leaves me as the only target. But why?" He asked looking from George to Eden.

"Mosely thinks highly of himself." George said, "And you did get him quite angry the other night. He may have asked the German to get rid of you out of spite."

A young woman in a Wren uniform knocking at the open door suddenly interrupted them.

"Excuse me sir, but the duty officer asked that I bring you these messages. He saw you had arrived and thought they might be important." She said timidly. When she saw George's face she involuntarily threw her empty hand to her mouth and gasped audibly.

George smiled and winked at her.

Eden stood and walked over to take the messages she held in her other hand.

"That's all right, Miss Collins. Tell the officer on duty I'll have a look at them." He said as he gently ushered her out the doorway and closed the door. He looked down at the top message as he walked back to his desk and suddenly stopped. He lifted the message from the small stack and read it more closely.

"What is it Anthony?" Harry said turning to look at Eden.

"Mosely is dead. His body was found in the charred remains of his home. Inspectors won't know if it was accidental or not until tomorrow." Eden said looking up at both men.

"I'll bet it was no accident." George mumbled.

"Seems quite a coincidence don't you think?' Harry asked. "I mean, He's in the link to what happened to me," He looked at George then corrected himself, "I mean us. What time did it happen?"

"The fire brigade received a call from a neighbor around midnight. The neighbor said he heard an explosion and when he looked out of his bedroom window to see if the bombing had begun again, he saw Mosely's home in flames." Eden said reading from the message.

"That means we won't be able to question him." Harry said glumly, and then brightened.

"One of the gunmen gave us the street where the house Schellenberg is living is located. It was Victoria Park wasn't it George" Harry asked looking to George. George nodded.

"We'll have to wait until morning. Without an address we'll need to go house to house." Eden said, continuing over to his desk. He perched on the desktop again and picked up the next message.

"Harry, you are going to leave the search to me. I received official notification from the Germans of their arrival tomorrow. As to how many or where they'll start, I don't know." he said.

"That makes it imperative we get to Bletchley tomorrow." Harry said then looking at George he added, "You'll need to find George another uniform. His was left in the ruins of the house."

Eden looked up from the message he was still reading, ready to read the riot act to George but with one look at the man, his face and his clothes, he stopped.

"I'll get Miss Collins on it." Eden said. Seeing George's puzzled look, he added, "We keep a small supply room now. The guards often stay in the cellar between shifts and from time to time require repairs or replacement items for their uniforms. Sergeant isn't it?"

George nodded and replied, "Wouldn't happen to have a pay book down there to go with sergeants rank would you?"

Eden glared at George. George shrugged in response and looked down at the floor sheepishly.

"You'll need to get a hold of Donovan to let him know the news." Harry said.

"I'll send a messenger over. Let me go and take care of the uniform and I'll send the messenger." Eden replied, rising from the desk and started to walk out of the room.

"You better make it a battle dress uniform. You sent a dress uniform last time. A lorry driver would hardly be dressed up." Harry yelled after him.

"Your face looks like hell George ol' boy. You better get some rest. Tomorrow is going to be a big day." Harry said as he looked over to George.

"Today you mean, according to clock on Eden's desk, we have about three hours until sunrise. What time do you plan on heading up to Bletchley?" George asked as he rose from the chair. He walked over to the bookcase and looked at the titles.

"With the Germans due in, I'd like to get an early start. Bletchley may be high on their list as places they want to cover." Harry answered.

Seeing George browsing the books he asked, "You're a fairly learned man aren't you?"

George turned from the bookcase and looked at Harry. He walked back to his chair and sat.

"I come from a pretty rough part of town. Where I grew up learning was done in the streets. You had to survive. I was one of the few who liked school though. My chums didn't think that was great. I got in a lot of fights just by saying I wanted to go to the library instead of nosing around the wharves, trying to steal whatever was handy. As I grew up, I got bigger and the fighting stopped. I still went to the library every chance I got. It left me a kind of loner. When my da died, I had to go to work on the docks to feed the family. I dropped out of school and lost any chance of going on to university." George paused and glanced at the bookshelf. Staring at it for a moment he turned back to Harry.

"I kept on reading late at night. It made no difference really, in my line of work, but I could chat away with the sailors that came in from different countries. I taught myself Finnish, Italian and French. One day my Mother said I was loosing my cockney accent and talking like one the bankers." George chuckled at this and Harry smiled.

"You would have thought I told her I was a fairy or something!" George continued. "She had grown up along the river as had my da. The rough life was all she knew. One day Lord Mosely was down on the docks looking for a shipment that was supposed to come in from Germany. He came to me. I found the crate. It had been set aside as undeliverable because all the labeling had worn off. We chatted a little and the next thing I know he offers me a job. Says I'd be perfect as his manservant. He offered a little more money than I was making at the docks and a better part of town to live in, so I took him up on it." George finished by shaking his head as if to indicate he had been a fool.

"Being a manservant turned out to be little more than a bodyguard?" Harry asked.

"Yeah, but more like a lackey. I did the shopping, ran errands and once in awhile I scared the hell out of people he wanted scared. Never hurt anyone though. He had his BFU friends for the tough jobs."

"Well, now you're a British soldier!" Harry grinned across to George.

"Really moving up in the world aren't I!" George smiled back.

Eden entered the room.

"Miss Collins will deliver a uniform to you later." He said to George as he walked back to his desk. As he sat in the chair he turned to Harry.

"A messenger has been dispatched to Donovan. I told him briefly what happened tonight and told him to move his timetable up. I also had a cellar room setup so you gentlemen can get some sleep. I suggest you get to bed now. Tomorrow is going to be a long day. I'll have someone wake you by, let's see," Eden said as he looked at the clock on his desk. "By nine. Is that satisfactory?" He asked looking up at Harry.

"I was hoping to get going a little earlier but considering the late hour, nine is fine." Harry said as he stood. Grabbing the bag he headed for the door. George followed.

"Oh, and Harry," Eden stopped them, "Miss Collins will bring you a change of clothes and a uniform also. Two sets of ID will be given to you both in the morning. Just tell the sentry at the cellar door who you are and he'll show you to your room." Eden spoke as he rose from the chair. "I'm terribly sorry about Agnes, Harry, I truly am." He added.

Harry felt a pang in his stomach at the mention of Agnes. He nodded to Eden and he and George left the office.

The cellar room was not much bigger than a large closet but it fit two standard army issue cots. Harry set the bag on the floor, removed his shoes and rolled unto the cot. He was asleep in minutes.

#

As Harry and George fell asleep, three Heinkle Airplanes readied were being loaded at Berlin Templehof airport. 225 German administrators, Gestapo and Abwehr agents prepared to begin the occupation of England. One thousand army troops would arrive later that day followed by ships carrying ten thousand more the next day.

CHAPTER 13

Donovan woke George and Harry at precisely 9 o'clock. The uniforms and change of clothes were hung inside the door. As Harry and George dressed in the uniforms, Donovan updated them.

· "The German's arrived before dawn this morning. They've got all the officials jumping through their asses. The first place they went was to the Intelligence building. Eden has some official up in his office now."

Harry stopped buttoning his shirt and looked to Donovan.

"They don't know about us do they?" He asked.

"No. I have the truck parked on Downing Street. The driver is an old friend of mine from the SAS. He loaded the truck with some dummy boxes and a few select weapons. Hopefully you won't need the guns but better safe than sorry. I'll take you to the truck when your finished dressing."

"No rash of bacon and muffins this morning?" George grumbled. His face wasn't as swollen but he still looked like hell.

Donovan laughed and took two items from his pocket.

"Here are two razors and I brought a bucket of water. Over there. "He pointed to a tin bucket in the corner. "It's probably cold water by now. But you'll need to shave at least while in uniform. I'm going to check the situation and be right back" Donovan exited the room and closed the door.

117

Harry picked up the razor, looked at George and then at the bucket. Shrugging his shoulders he started to undo the shirt buttons. George felt the cuts on his face and grimaced.

Donovan returned in half an hour. Both men were ready.

"I got some news from Mrs. Boatwright. She says the Germans sent a couple of guys to Bletchley and hour ago. You'll need to be extra careful, fellas." Donovan said as he grabbed Harry's bag. "She's pretty tore up about Agnes too, Harry. I was sorry to hear the news myself." He added.

Harry nodded and walked into the hall. He had stuffed the extra clothes into the bag and transferred the fuses and explosives to his pant pocket. He had stuffed the gun into the back waistband under his uniform coat. The pockets bulged some with the explosive but the coat was long enough to hide the bulk of it.

When they were out on the street headed for the lorry, Harry asked, "What about Churchill?"

"He was my first stop when I heard the Germans had arrived. I took him out in the truck and he is now waiting in an apartment of a friend of mine in Wapping. Eden looks to be in trouble so I'll take a sedan from the motor pool and deliver Churchill myself to Bletchley. We'll meet you under the railway bridge off Albion Street. That idea of a double was pure genius. I was even fooled when the fool answered the door. I explained to him the ex Prime Minister doesn't answer the door his butler does. Hopefully he won't make the same mistake when the Germans come calling."

Harry nodded as he walked.

When they reached the truck, a well-built sergeant jumped from the driver's seat and saluted. Harry stared at him for a moment and Donovan finally nudged him. Harry forgot he was in a colonel's uniform and belatedly returned the salute.

"Harry, this Master Sergeant Boothe." Donavon said by way of introduction.

Harry shook the sergeant's hand. "This is Sergeant Hayes." He said looking over to George. "He's new to the Army."

Boothe looked puzzled as he shook George's hand.

"I'll explain on the way." Harry said noticing the look on Boothe's face.

Donovan pushed the bag into the back of the truck under the canvas. The three soldiers climbed in.

"On Albion then." Donovan said to Harry as he shut the truck door for Boothe.

"On Albion." Harry gave a small salute and turning to Boothe said. "Let's go."

It was a tight fit in the truck. Harry was sandwiched in between the two big men and had to crunch his legs up as Boothe shifted gears.

"This is going to be a long ride." He groaned as Boothe shifted again.

As they turned on Wilton Avenue in Bletchley, Harry finished going over the plan. They pulled up to the gate at the end of the street. A guard peered into the truck and seeing Harry saluted. Harry returned the salute and all three handed the guard their IDs. A second guard opened the back of the truck and inspected the boxes. Satisfied he closed the canvas flap.

"Delivery?" The guard asked as he handed the Ids back.

"These two are delivering. I hitched a ride. I'm here to do an inspection for MI." Harry answered.

The guard nodded and waved them through. They drove up the road to the mansion. Harry was struck by the ugliness of it. It seemed as if the architect couldn't make up his mind. A round tower-like structure stood out on the left while, gables, battlements, bay windows and other assorted architectures made up the rest of the building. The red brick just made it look more odd.

George moved to allow Harry out.

"Like one of those gangster mansions in American movies." He said as Harry straightened his uniform and let the blood flow back into his legs.

"You don't see the charm?" He said to George as he started to the cathedral-like arch that was the main entrance.

George smiled and got back in the truck. Boothe drove them past what had been the tennis courts and around the back of the building.

Another sentry at the main entrance met Harry. The man saluted and barely glanced at Harry's identification before opening the door.

The main hall was adorned in oak paneling and looked more like a hunting lodge than a country manor. There were people milling about, entering and exiting the many doors that lined the far wall. Harry walked over to a desk that appeared to be some sort of reception. A young woman in a Wren's uniform looked up and smiled. "Can I help you sir?" She asked.

"I'm Colonel Lloyd from MI5. I'm here to do an inspection before the arrival of the German administrators." Harry smiled back and looked around to see if there were any Germans present.

"You're a bit late, sir. The Germans have been here for a couple of hours now." She frowned.

"Have they begun their inspection yet?" Harry questioned, trying to hide his anxiety.

"No. They've been upstairs with Commander Denniston and Mr. Knox since they arrived."

"Well then, don't bother the Director. I'll just have a look around and send him a copy of my report when I finish." Harry smiled at the Wren.

Blushing, she replied, "I can have Major Jennings escort you if you wish. He is our security chief."

"That would be fine." Harry said, knowing that if he declined, the suspicion would be too great.

"Just a moment." The Wren replied as she rose and walked across the hall to a door on the far wall.

She returned a short time later, with a small red-haired man in a major's uniform following her. The man approached Harry and extended his hand.

"I thought they would call off the inspection now that the Huns are here." He said amicably as he shook Harry's hand.

"The 'Huns' as you say, are our new allies, major." Harry admonished the man, testing his reaction.

The major's face turned the color of his hair. He coughed and replied, "Yes sir. No disrespect meant."

"Yes. Well then, let's get started before the bastards interrupt." Harry smilingly replied.

Surprised, the Major tried to suppress a smile then stammered, "Yes, sir! Where would you like to begin?"

"I imagine a place like this requires a lot of supplies. How are supplies delivered?"

"In the back. We have a small loading dock with a small warehouse in the cellar. Mostly administrative stuff gets delivered here. Paper, pens and the like."

"Well, let's start there Major." Harry said.

"Yes sir. Follow me." The Major led Harry across the hall towards a large ornate staircase. Behind the staircase a hall wound to the back of the building. The Major and Harry followed this hall. When they approached the back Harry saw an opened large overhead door and on the dock were George and Boothe. The lorry was backed up to the dock and the men along with a man from the mansion were unloading the boxes.

The Major seemed alarmed and excused himself as he approached Boothe. He spoke to Boothe while moving his hands and arms about. After a short discussion, he returned to where Harry stood.

"A problem Major?" Harry asked.

"No. I just didn't expect a delivery today. It seems the Germans have asked to have some papers moved here. This transition is going to make my job a nightmare!" the Major shook his head and pointed back down the hall. "If you don't mind, sir, I'll show you the cellar and the storeroom."

Harry nodded and as he turned to follow the Major as he headed down the hall, he touched his forehead in a quick salute to Boothe. Boothe had acted exceptionally. Donovan could sure pick his men.

Halfway back down the hallway, the major turned and opened a door. He reached in and flicked on a light. Harry could see a short set of stairs that led below. He followed the major as he descended.

The cellar was divided by the walkway. Doors and cages lined either side. The fourth door on the left, Harry knew from the blueprints, held the Enigma machine. At the far end the Major stopped and opened a cage.

"Here is the storeroom sir. As you can see, we have no shortages here." The major said sweeping his arm to display the neat shelves lined with paper, carbons, pens and other assorted office supplies. Against the far wall, boxes were neatly stacked and labeled.

Harry took a perfunctory glance around the room and nodded. "Looks to be well maintained. Good order to it." He said. His mind was on how to get into the Enigma room without raising too much suspicion. He had the letter from Eden he could show but he didn't know how much the Major knew about the Enigma. As security chief, he should be in on the loop but Harry wasn't certain.

Harry stepped back into the hall and the Major followed. Boothe, George and the other man were coming down the stairs at the other end, carrying boxes.

Harry purposely walked up the hall and stopped at he door to the Enigma, where he backed against it to allow the men to pass. The Major stopped several feet back.

As the Major approached, Harry stepped back and pointed to the door and the heavy padlock securing it.

"What's in here?" He asked.

"Top secret, sir. I can't show you that unless I have higher authority."

"I see." Harry reached into his inside breast pocket and extracted the letter. "Will this do?" He asked as he handed it to the puzzled Major.

The Major opened it and read it. He scrutinized Harry for a moment, and then reached into his pocket, bringing out a set of keys.

"From the foreign minister himself, huh?' That's good enough for me." He said as he unlocked the door and opened it. Harry just got a glance inside when he heard a crash from the hallway. He turned and saw that the men had dropped their boxes as they tried to maneuver them into the storeroom.

"Looks as if they have made a mess of your storeroom, Major." Harry said nodding towards the end of the hallway.

The Major swung around and saw the commotion. "Bloody hell!" he cried as he ran toward the men and the mess.

Harry quickly pulled a fuse and small piece of explosive from his pocket. Following the Major, he stuck the fuse into the putty.

The major, cursing the ineptitude of the men, started picking up boxes and straightening the mess.

Harry covertly placed the explosive into George's hand and whispered, "Give me ten minutes then set the fuse. Stick it amongst the papers in there somewhere. On your next trip, bring an empty box and stop at that door you saw me leaning against."

George nodded and took the putty, sliding it into his pocket.

"Major, We better get back there. You left the door unlocked." Harry motioned up the hall.

"Damn!" The Major exploded, then to the men, "get this cleaned up!" He then rushed out of the room and up the hall to the Enigma room.

Harry followed and entered the room. To his surprise he saw not one but several Enigmas. There were boxes filled with wheels and what looked like codebooks. Against one wall were some cans marked cleaning solvent.

"Do you know what these are Colonel?" The Major asked.

"Yes, I do. I just hope the Germans don't find them." Harry said as he opened one of the wooden cases and looked closely at one of the machines. It had a keyboard like a typewriter with a telephone switch-type plug board on the front. Three round gear-like wheels stuck up on the top of the box. He closed it; satisfied it matched the picture he had.

"Major, I'm going to let you in on a very top secret. After I tell you, you'll have two choices: cooperate or die." Harry said as he pulled the gun from under his coat.

The astonished Major instinctively reached for his sidearm but knew the effort was futile. He looked at Harry, cocked his head and asked, "What's the secret? I hope you aren't planning on telling the Germans about these."

Harry shook his head.

"No. I need to make sure they do not find out about them at all. I also must take one with me. Are you going to help or are you going to die?" Harry emphasized his question by raising the gun and pointing at the Major's head.

Harry was impressed. The Major didn't even blink. He looked at Harry then at the boxes. Finally he said, "How are we going to get them out?"

Harry lowered the gun and nodded at the Major's side arm. "Take it out and set it on the floor." The Major complied and went one step further by sliding it towards Harry.

"I'm not going to try and stop you." The Major said. "I've been worried about these myself since the Germans arrived. I know what happened to the fellows who worked these machines, by the way."

"I had nothing to do with that," Harry said. "My job is to get one of these and the plans to the Bombe out of here. Where are the plans by the way?"

"They were locked up a couple doors down. This morning I moved them in here." The Major moved two boxes to reveal four cardboard tubes behind them.

"Harry put his gun back behind his coat and smiled at the major. "Good job! It will make things easier."

He walked over and lifted the tubes out and set them upright against one of the Enigma boxes. He turned as George dropped a box at the door.

"Colonel. We have company." George said as he stepped aside. A tall man dressed in a black uniform stepped from behind the door into the room.

"What have we here gentlemen?" The German said as he looked around the room. "Well, well! Looks as if you have a collection of our most secret weapon. Berlin will not be pleased."

The German walked over and flipped open the top of one of the Enigma boxes. He turned to Harry.

"Colonel. I won't ask how you got these but I need to know if this is all of them." The German smiled but his eyes were stone cold.

Harry looked at George and nodded slightly towards the Major's gun on the floor.

"This is all of them. Never could figure out how they work but it sure kept us busy." Harry answered, moving closer to the German.

The German stepped back suddenly grunted and fell to the floor as George hit him in the neck from behind.

"Couldn't chance having a gunshot overheard" George explained as he dragged the body between two boxes.

Harry nodded and grabbing one of the Enigma boxes, he placed into the box in the doorway. "Grab the plans Major and let's get this out to the lorry!"

"What about these others?" The major asked as he picked up the tubes.

Harry set the big box down and reached into his pocket. He heard a popping sound come from the end of the hallway and knew the explosive had detonated in the storeroom.

"George, pour the cleaning solvent in those cans on the German and boxes and then set the explosive." He said as he tossed first the putty then a fuse to George.

George grabbed a can of solvent and began to pour it over the German. The German jerked and sputtered as he started to come to. George kicked him in the back of the head and the German fell silent again.

Boothe arrived and helped Harry carry the box from the cellar, followed by the Major.

They secured the packages behind the boxes left in the lorry.

"You'll have to stay and delay any kind of attempt at putting out the fire." Harry said to the Major.

The major, tight lipped, nodded. He turned and started for the hallway. After a couple of steps he turned back and saluted Harry.

Harry smiled grimly and returned the salute. The Major turned on his heels and retreated back into the building as George came out.

Harry patted Boothe on the shoulder and turned to go around the truck. 'Let's go before they discover the fire and shut this place down." He shouted.

They drove away from the mansion and towards the main gate. The sentry just waved as they passed. Harry heard George exhale in relief.

"Now to get Churchill and be on our way to Ireland." Harry said as he dodged another one of Boothe's gearshifts.

Behind them they heard a loud explosion and George looked out the window back to the Mansion. A huge cloud of smoke rose from the building and he could see flames shooting from some of the windows.

He leaned back in the truck and turned to Harry.

"Little more bang than I thought." He said.

Harry was just as surprised by the explosion. He hadn't thought it was that powerful.

"Confined space, fumes from the solvent, they all contributed to the blast." Boothe explained. "Considering the old timbers holding the place up, I don't think there will be anything identifiable left."

"Let's hope not." Harry leaned forward and pointed. "There's the bridge."

Boothe turned left under the bridge. Donovan was standing just out-side the shadow of the bridge, looking at the cloud of smoke behind them. The sedan was parked at the curb.

As the truck came to a stop, Donovan ran up to the passenger door. He had to jump back as George opened the door and jumped out.

"What the hell happened Harry?" Donovan enquired, somewhat out of breath. "It was supposed to be a small fire!"

Harry slid across the seat and jumped out next to George.

"We ran into a complication. Namely a German discovered the machines. We did what we could under the circumstances." Harry gave Donovan a steely stare, challenging him to argue the point further.

Donovan changed subjects.

"Eden has been arrested, along with a half dozen other Churchill cabinet members. They krauts were on the way to Chartwell when we left." Donovan said, glancing at the sedan. "It won't be long before they figure out that the man at Chartwell is a fraud." He added.

"George, you and Boothe transfer the packages to the boot of the sedan. We'll take it the rest of the way. It'll be a lot faster, not to mention a lot more comfortable." Harry said as he started for the sedan.

He stopped half way and looked at the billowing smoke coming from the direction of the mansion. His mind quickly thought of the Major and the young Wren. "I hope they made it out okay." He said to himself as he continued to the sedan.

Churchill opened the back door as Harry approached.

"Looks as if you got your fire Harry. Good to see you made it out okay." Churchill said as he swung his legs out as if to exit the sedan.

"Stay were you are Mr. Churchill. We don't need anyone recognizing you." Harry said as he hurried to shield the open door from the street.

Comprehending, Churchill slid back into the car.

"We're going to take the sedan the rest of the way. Sergeant Hayes will transfer the packages to the boot. Then we'll be on our way." Harry said as he leaned into the back of the car.

Donovan approached the car and spoke, "Harry, I have a message here. I believe it's from your Irish Uncle. Some hoodlum looking fellow gave it to me outside of the foreign ministry offices."

Harry took the message and opened it. Sean briefly sent his regards and told Harry he should visit Wales while he was in England. He suggested Barmouth as being especially nice. Sean finished by adding that he hoped an opportunity would arise where they could get together again.

"Good news?" Donovan asked.

"Do you know where Barmouth is?" Harry looked up at Donovan.

"In Wales, on the coast. A nice little town. Nice beaches. A bit off the beaten path though." Churchill interrupted.

Harry turned back to Churchill. "How far from here?"

"Oh four or five hours, I'd say." Churchill replied.

Harry turned to Donovan. "Change of plans. I'm going to head for Wales. If the German's are planning on closing borders I'd think Wales would be the last if at all."

"Is there ferry service from there to Ireland? How do you propose to get across?" Donovan asked.

"I have a hunch I may have some relatives in the area who may help." Harry answered as he turned to watch George and Boothe finish loading the Enigma box and Bombe plans into the back of the car.

George retrieved two petrol cans from the back of the lorry along with two rifles. He put the items into the back and closed the boot. He and Boothe walked around to where Harry and Donovan stood.

Harry turned to Boothe.

"Sergeant, it has been a pleasure. If I ever have a need for anyone to help me out of jamb, you're the first I'll call." He said as he grasped Boothe's hand and placed his other hand on his shoulder.

Boothe smiled warmly, stepped back and saluted. "Thank you sir. It's been a pleasure. Mr. Donovan will know where to find me if need be." With that Boothe turned and retreated to the lorry.

"Harry, I need to get back. I forgot to add that your friend Schellenberg has taken over the German mission here. I'd keep a close eye out. I don't know what he knows but he may come after you. Especially if he can't find you where you should be."

"I'll watch my back. Thanks for all the help, Bill." Harry replied as he took Donovan's hand. Donovan shook his hand, leaned into the car and said something to Churchill then followed Boothe to the lorry.

Harry and George watched as the lorry roared off down Albion Street.

"Let's get moving George. Head Northwest into Wales." Harry climbed into the back with Churchill while George climbed into the driver seat, started the engine and headed for the main road to North Hampton.

CHAPTER 14

Churchill was eager to learn the details and Harry tiredly obliged. When Harry finished, they continued on in silence.

Churchill stole a glance at Harry. Harry had laid his head back and had fallen fast asleep. "There is much more to this man that is visibly apparent." Churchill thought. He showed no outward emotion even after all he had been through. He didn't know Harry all that well but he felt immensely secure in his capable care. Churchill settled back in the seat and watched the English countryside roll by.

A half-hour out of Birmingham, Harry awoke. He was thirsty and very hungry.

"Find a pub somewhere along here, George. I'm famished and I imagine you are too." He leaned forward as he spoke.

"Sounds good. I'm a bit worn out. Maybe a small meal and some coffee will liven me up a bit." George said, glad to have the long silence broken.

Harry turned to Churchill, who appeared to be dozing. He surprised Harry by opening his eyes as he said, "Just grab me a sandwich and a bottle of Ale. I don't believe it would be wise for me to be seen."

"I was going to suggest that. George and I also need to get out of uniform. We'll be less conspicuous ourselves that way." Harry said as he leaned back.

A few minutes later, George pulled the sedan into the parking area in front of a small pub. Harry scrambled out and stretched. The building stood alone surrounded by trees. A green hill rose gently behind the pub. A gray sign hung above the entrance. It proclaimed the place to be 'Sheep's Rest'.

George exited the car and opened the boot. He extracted the bag given to them by Donovan and walked around to the passenger door.

As he opened it he said to Harry, "May as well change now. After I'm done I'll refuel the car while you change."

Harry nodded, and took a few steps away from the car, surveying the area. No other cars were in the parking lot, which was not unusual considering the wartime gas rationing. He wondered if the place was open. He decided to check the door.

The door was solid wood and he couldn't see through the heavily curtained window next to it. He tried the handle and the door opened easily. An older man stood behind the bar wiping glasses. He looked up as Harry leaned in.

"Just checking to see if you're open." Harry said smiling as he stepped into the doorway.

The publican nodded and replied, "Can't make any money keeping the door locked. Although I don't get much business these days, stragglers such as yourself are always welcome."

"My companion and I will be in a moment." Harry waved as he stepped back outside and closed the door.

George, now dressed in a brown wool sweater and dark gray pants was emptying a petrol can into the tank of the sedan as Harry returned and climbed in the open passenger door.

A few minutes later, George and Harry, now dressed similar to George, entered the pub and walked up to the bar. The publican had just stepped back behind the bar from a small door. He eyed Harry suspiciously, noticing the change in clothes, but quickly brightened into a grin.

"Thought you might be hungry. I just turned on the stove." He said by way of explanation. "Don't have much, war and all." He said "But I

132 Desperate Times

can manage some fried eggs and some bacon. Got my own animals out back." He winked.

"Would it be possible to get three egg sandwiches and maybe a pint to go?" Harry asked as he pulled out a stool and sat at the bar. George did the same.

"In a rush?" The man asked.

"Have to make it to Edinburgh before dark." Harry answered nonchalantly.

"Bit of a ways to travel gents." The man said as he set two mugs in front of the men. He reached under the bar and produced two bottles. "Afraid, the tap isn't connected. Stuff goes flat if it isn't pumped regularly." He said.

As the publican turned and exited through the small door, Harry turned on his stool and looked the interior over. It was a typical small pub like thousands all over England. The wooden walls were dark with years of smoke. Pictures with hunting scenes and meadows lined the walls on all sides. There were four tables with chairs set in the middle of the room. On one of the tables, Harry saw a newspaper.

Harry retrieved the paper and saw it was this morning's issue of the London Times. The headline proclaimed:'Armistice Terms Begin!' below the banner in smaller print —'Germans arrive to begin fulfilling the terms of the agreement'

Harry carried the paper back to the bar and sat next to George.

"Looks as if we timed this just right. Another day and we would have been up against more than just one Nazi at Bletchley." He said to George.

George leaned over and scanned the front page. He frowned, leaned closer and said, "Says German troops will be deploying around Great Britain in the next few days. I thought this was a friendly armistice?"

Harry looked at the other man and George could see his blue eyes had turned into a steely stare.

"I have a feeling we've been sold out George. The people have been lied to." Harry shook the paper in his hands. "We're to go the way of

Poland and Czechoslovakia after all. Not a word in here from anyone in government."

"You thinking the Germans got to the press already?" George asked, "I don't think they had time to get their propaganda in the paper so soon. I mean, they just arrived this morning." He took a swallow of the ale.

The publican entered the bar carrying a tray with three egg sandwiches and a half a loaf of fresh bread. He set it on the bar in front of them.

Harry pushed the glass in front of him towards the barman and shook his head. "I better stick to tea if you have it. I'm driving." He said to the barman.

"Suit yourself. I'll get a cup." He turned and exited back through the door.

Harry picked up the conversation as he reached for a sandwich. "I don't think the Germans needed to take over the press. The papers have been calling for an end to the war for a few weeks now. I think they'll blindly print what is ever passed to them by the government, now that Churchill is gone." He took a bite of the sandwich and was surprised at just how hungry he was. Dropping the conversation, he finished the sandwich. George started on his and they ate together in silence.

The man returned with a cup and set it front of Harry. He eyed their empty plates and then studied the two men closely. It was rather suspicious that a man first enters dressed as a colonel then returns dressed in civilian a few minutes later. The other one was big and appeared to be watching everything around him, as if suspecting someone may surprise him. Could they be Germans? He wondered. Deciding to draw them out, he spoke.

"Heard on the BBC a few minutes ago that the Germans have requested the arrest of Churchill. What do think of that?" He said, watching the men's reactions.

Harry successfully fought the urge to look at George. Instead he looked up at the barman and fixed him with a suspicious stare.

"I'd say I hope the ol' boy out runs 'em." He said.

George nodded and added, "It's criminal enough that we signed an armistice with the Nazis. To arrest a man who had been doing his job would be a travesty."

The barman suspected something was going on with the pair, but he was satisfied it have anything to do with the Germans. The smaller man's hard look was enough to say that the man had his own reservations about him.

"I'm going to ask right out. Why the change in clothes?" He asked Harry as he placed the empty plates back on the tray. He took the extra sandwich, set it between Harry and George, and looked at Harry expectantly.

"I had official business to attend to earlier and now I'm off duty." Harry said matter-of-factly. He glanced down at the paper then back to the barman.

"And what do you think of the present situation, Mr.—?" Harry asked.

"Owens, Thomas Owens." The barman answered and reached over the bar to shake Harry's hand.

"Harry Lloyd and this is George Hayes." He said taking the hand.

George nodded as he shook the barman's hand.

"Well, Mr. Lloyd, I don't think Mr. Attlee and his friends did us any favors. I know, out here, with the exception of rationing and the loss of customers, we haven't had to suffer the effects of war. I realize it must have been hell in the cities, but dammit, you don't just quit. You can't just hand them the damn country without a fight." Owens punctuated his statements by pounding his right fist into his open left palm.

"I feel the same way. But we put Attlee there and now we must suffer the consequences." George said.

"I heard the French have developed some sort of underground fighting organization they call the resistance. I plan on joining one here if it can get established." Owens said as he leaned onto the bar.

"That could be very dangerous, Mr. Owens. The Germans aren't fighting anyone on a large scale now. They could easily send troops here to crush any kind of local uprisings." Harry pointed out.

"That won't be for long. I also heard on the BBC that the Americans have given the German government 72 hours to issue a formal apology and reparations for the sinking of their ship a couple of days ago. The Germans, at least not Hitler, aren't going to issue an apology to anyone. The yanks will be in it for sure now." Owens said with a look of satisfaction on his face.

This time Harry couldn't squelch the urge and turned to look at George with arched eyebrows.

George pursed his lips and shrugged at Harry.

"What else has the BBC had to say?" Harry asked as turned back to Owens.

"Well, mostly about the Germans arriving. A few administrators today, a few more tomorrow and then a few thousand troops by weeks end. All civilian travel out of the country has been suspended until the Germans are in place." Owens shrugged.

"Does that include England to Wales or Scotland?" Harry asked anxiously.

"Didn't say. All neutral ships have until tomorrow to leave British waters. I guess they didn't want anyone leaving with them." Owens said as he took the tray. He started for the door then turned around.

"I'll put together some more sandwiches for you two and fill a jug of tea you can take with you." He said over his shoulder as continued through the door.

"If they're looking for Churchill and closing the borders, we could be in big trouble here, Harry." George said balefully.

Harry turned to the outside door for a minute, thinking, and then turned back to George.

"We'll have to cross at an out of the way place. They'll be less likely to have the news yet and if they have heard and stop us, we'll have less trouble eliminating the problem." Harry finally replied.

Mr. Owens entered again with a bag and a large sealed jug. He set it on the bar in front of Harry and said.

"I have my suspicions about you two. But if my instincts are right, your welcome here anytime."

Harry took out some bills and set them on the bar. He grabbed the bag and stood.

"Thanks, Mr. Owens. I don't know if we'll be back by this way again, but if we are, we'll be sure to stop." He said as reached over the bar offering a handshake.

Owens shook hands with Harry then with George as George took the other sandwich, swallowed the remainder of his glass and headed for the door.

"Keep your money, Harry. Your company was pay enough." Owens said as he took the bills from the bar and reached over to put them into Harry's hand.

Harry, caught by surprise, didn't protest. He turned and followed George to the exit.

Thomas Owens watched the two men close the door then hurried to the window to watch them leave. He pulled the curtain back in time to see Harry hand the bag and jug to someone in the back of the car. George opened the passenger door, said something to the man in back then closed the door. As Harry closed the back door and started around the car, Thomas caught a glimpse of the back passenger as the passenger's bulldog face peered out.

"Mary Mother of Jesus!" Thomas gasped as recognition set in. He hurriedly closed the curtain and sat heavily into the nearest chair.

CHAPTER 15

As Harry and George ate, General Schellenberg's staff car with minia-ture red swastika flags adorning the fenders pulled through the gates at Bletchley. The scene that greeted him was chaotic. Emergency vehicles still surrounded the charred mansion and hundreds of spectators milled about the grounds. The SS driver brought the car to a stop about 75 yards from the ruined building. Schellenberg emerged from the car and stared at the ruined building. After a minute he turned and scanned the crowd. Seeing two British officers standing near the front of a group of people, he approached.

"What has happened here?" Schellenberg demanded.

"Some sort of explosion occurred in the cellar. Nobody has been able to enter the building to determine what caused it." Commander Denniston stepped forward and answered. He was watching Schellenberg closely out of the corner of his eye as he looked past him to the car. He wasn't too keen on having some Nazi mucking about the place.

Schellenberg turned and eyed the commander. "You are?" he asked.

"Commander Denniston, I'm in charge of the Government Code and Cipher School." Denniston said, nodding at the mansion. He turned to get a better look at the German. He certainly didn't look like a member of the superior race, he thought. The long overcoat hung on the General like it was two sizes too big; his face was thin and he had a skinny chicken neck. Denniston took an immediate dislike to the German officer.

"Where is Hauptman Moeller?" Schellenberg demanded as he returned Denniston's scrutiny.

"The officer that arrived this morning has not been seen since the explosion." Denniston replied.

"How many others are not accounted for?" Schellenberg enquired as he turned his gaze to the crowd on the grounds.

"We have been trying to determine that. So far we have four of our personnel unaccounted for." Denniston answered, then added: "Are there more of your people we should be aware of?"

Schellenberg ignored the question.

"Where is your head of security? Has he been questioned?" Schellenberg turned and looked at the officer standing behind Denniston.

Denniston turned and waved Major Jennings forward. Jennings looked terrible. His uniform was torn and full of soot and his head had a bandage above the left eye.

Jennings saluted and said "Major Jennings, sir. Chief of security."

Schellenberg stared at Jennings with a cold expression until Jennings, intimidated, dropped his salute.

"How could this happen, Major? Is this a terrorist bombing? A place such as this should be highly secured. "

"It is, or was, sir. Nobody could get in without careful examination of his papers by two separate entry points." Jennings replied, lowering his eyes to avoid the hard look of Schellenberg.

"How do you explain a sabotage act such as this?" The German bellowed waving his arm towards the mansion.

"Sabotage? No one knows if it was sabotage or not. For all we know, the damn furnace blew up!" Jennings burst out.

Denniston raised his eyebrows at the outburst.

"You will contain your emotions Major and treat me with the respect of a senior officer!" Schellenberg admonished.

Jennings didn't reply, but he pursed his lips and looked back at the ground.

"When did you last see Hauptman Moeller?" Schellenberg asked.

"I last saw him entering the door to the cellar off of the back hall about ten minutes before the explosion." Jennings lied.

Schellenberg squinted at Jennings and spat back "Are you implying my officer had something to do with this?"

"I'm implying nothing. I'm just telling you what I saw." Jennings said defiantly.

"It's true sir," the Wren who had worked the reception desk stepped forward and interrupted. "I saw the German officer go towards the back hallway only a few minutes before the explosion."

All three men turned and looked at her. Jennings tried to warn her off using his eyes. She either didn't see him or ignored him, for she went on: "It was about twenty minutes after you and Colonel Lloyd went that way, sir." She was looking at Jennings but Jennings turned away to look at Schellenberg.

Schellenberg's head shot up at the mention of Lloyd's name.

"Harold Lloyd? Of MI5?" He asked, looking from Jennings to the Wren.

Jennings didn't answer but the Wren stepped up, "Yes sir, I mean I don't remember his first name but he was from MI5."

Jennings gave her a cold hard stare and tried to push her back. This time she caught the warning and voluntarily stepped back behind the commander and major.

"Now that is interesting!" Schellenberg said as he grasped his hands behind his back and looked at the major.

"What was his business here, Major?" he asked.

"He came to inspect in preparation for the Ger...er, your people's arrival." Jennings replied.

"Inspect? Why? Was he attempting to hide something from us?"

"No, sir. He said he wanted to make sure everything was in order for your arrival. We got to the loading dock and were on our way back to the cellar and the storeroom when the explosion occurred. I don't know what happened to him next. I scrambled to the front hall trying to get everyone out."

"You were with him when the explosion occurred? He was never out of your sight?" Schellenberg asked, not looking at Jennings but behind him to the Wren. She may know more than she has said, he thought.

"He was never out of my sight. And as I said, we were together in the back hall when the explosion occurred."

"Has his body been recovered?" Schellenberg asked as he turned his attention back to the major.

"We haven't done a search for survivors or victims yet. The fire officials haven't released the building to us." Denniston interjected.

"Who is handling this investigation?" Schellenberg turned to Denniston.

"Major Jennings will be once the authorities have given us the okay to search the rubble." Denniston replied as he nodded at Jennings.

"I will assign one of my own men to assist you, Major." Schellenberg said. He turned, looked at the building again and then started back to his car. He suddenly stopped and spun around, "Oh, and major, you will report to me personally this evening with the results of your investigation. I'll leave word where you can find me."

Without waiting for a reply, the German turned and continued to his car.

Denniston and Jennings watched as he sped away. Jennings turned and headed towards the mansion and the leader of the fire brigade. He had to get inside before his German assistant arrived.

#

Schellenberg sat in the back of the sedan brooding.

"Who was this Lloyd? Why did his name keep popping up?" He asked himself. Mosely had seemed to think he was a German sympathizer, but the SD had never heard of him. The Abwehr hadn't confirmed he worked for them, but that didn't mean he didn't. Canaris and his intelligence organization were at odds with the SD and if they had succeeded in getting someone on the inside of British Intelligence, they certainly wouldn't share that information with the SD. He'd have to get his personnel file from M5 and find out more about this man.

He knew the English had more than a code school at Bletchley. Spies had said the place was heavily guarded and had over a thousand people assigned. Moeller had been assigned to find out just what went on at the place, but now he had disappeared. The explosion had to be sabotage. For it to occur the day they arrived and during Lloyd's visit was too much of a coincidence.

If Lloyd's body wasn't amongst the rubble, then he had gotten away. But gotten away with what? What was the English hiding? He stretched out his legs under the front seat and closed his eyes as he contemplated the many questions this incident had conjured up. Perhaps the timid Major would have more answers tonight.

CHAPTER 16

It had taken the German General two hours to get one of his men out to assist Jennings. By the time he had arrived, Jennings had verified that all traces of the Enigma had been destroyed or removed. Denniston had hut 8, where the actual decrypting of Enigma messages was done, evacuated and all the documents contained in the building destroyed. Jennings had allowed the German corporal Schellenberg had sent to discover the remains of Hauptman Moeller. There wasn't much left of him. All that remained besides his blackened body was a charred boot, dagger and belt buckle.

The corporal had said Schellenberg would meet him at the foreign office building. As Jennings entered the building and made his way up to the foreign secretary's office, where the sentry had said the General was working, he wondered if colonel Lloyd and his package had safely arrived wherever it was they were going. He smiled as he reached up to knock on the office door.

#

Harry had driven the car on back roads from Birmingham, which had added an extra two hours to the journey, but they arrived safely in Barmouth as the sun was beginning to set.

The blackout had been lifted since the armistice and they could see the lights of the town before them and the harbor on the left as they crossed the bridge from Fairbourne. The spire of St. David's church loomed against the deep orange sky to their left.

"We'll scout out the hotel there to the right at the foot of the hills." Harry said pointed as turned right off the bridge.

"Remember our friend here." George said glancing over at the sleeping bulk of Churchill.

Churchill had admonished them for keeping him waiting in the car so long back at the little pub. He quieted down when he was offered the sandwiches but complained again about them forgetting his ale. He had regaled them about the history of the countryside as they had passed into Wales but had fallen silent, deep in thought shortly thereafter.

"I know. I'll check the place out to see if it has a back entrance for guests. If it does then we'll sneak him in that way after we get a room." Harry replied, as he turned left off of Panorama Road into the parking lot of the hotel.

"Why a room Harry? I had hoped we could find your Uncle and be on our way. The longer we hang about, the greater chance of someone spotting our friend here." George said.

"I don't intend to stay the night. We just need a place to hide Mr. Churchill and catch our breath until we can get out of here." Harry explained. "It may take a while to find Sean. We didn't exactly set a rendezvous. He may not arrive until later. I'm hoping word of the Germans arriving has reached Sean and he figures out we need to move quickly." Harry added as he glanced over to George.

George nodded his understanding but his furrowed brow told otherwise.

The sun was nearly set, leaving a dull orange glow along the horizon to the west. Clouds had been forming most of the afternoon and the smell of rain mixed with the sea was in the damp air. The breeze from the seashore was cold without the warmth of the sun and the exhaust of the car rose in wisps in the light of headlamps as the car came to a stop.

Harry left George and Churchill in the car and walked up to the entrance of the hotel. As he entered, he was surprised to see two uniformed German sailors walking through the lobby towards the noise of what must be a pub. He immediately backed out of the lobby and sped back to the car.

"There were German sailors in the lobby." He gasped as he started the car and headed away from the hotel.

An astonished George asked, "What the hell are Germans doing here? This place is too small and out of the way to be of any interest to Germans!"

"The sea, boys. They're probably from a ship that was sailing these waters and decided to see what Britain is all about now that the armistice is in effect." Churchill grumbled as he sat upright.

George looked at Churchill as if he were crazy.

"Hundreds of miles of coast and they pick the one town we head to. What are the odds on that?" He said to Churchill.

"Purely coincidence. Drive by the quay, Harry. Let's have a look at what kind of ship they have." Churchill said as he reached over the seat and tapped Harry on his shoulder.

Harry slowed as they neared the quay and pulled into the parking lot near the small boat dock. The German's vessel was easy to spot. It was the only boat along the quay that was lit up. It appeared to be a German E-boat. Fat, round hulled in front, the long boat had an open deck in back lined with metal rails. 20mm guns stood guard fore and aft. Two 21-inch torpedo tubes winged the front hull.

"Nasty little boats, those are. The Germans call them Schnellboots. They are equivalent to out motorized torpedo boats and they are quick little devils. They brought down a couple of destroyers at Dunkirk." Churchill, the former First Lord of the Admiralty expounded as they peered through the windshield at the boat.

Harry backed out of the parking lot and headed west along the shore road. Just past the train station he spotted another hotel. He parked the car and repeated his actions at the last hotel. This time the lobby was empty except for a young red headed woman behind the reception desk. He could here voices and laughter from a room he assumed to be a bar to his left as he walked across the lobby to the desk.

"I'm looking for a room with two beds. Have you any available?" He smiled at the girl.

She returned his smile warmly.

"Would you like an upstairs room or downstairs?" she asked.

"Downstairs if possible, near the back. I have an aged uncle traveling with me and he has a problem with too much noise." Harry said as he tilted his head toward the barroom. "Would you also have a back entrance? It would be much easier helping him to the room."

"Yes. We have a room available next to the back entrance. But a few of our guests use that door late at night. Sometimes they are a bit noisy after visiting the local pubs." She winked at Harry slyly.

"That will be fine. He has medication to help him sleep. Even the Blitz couldn't arouse him!" He joked as he signed the registry. He used a false name just in case.

The girl handed him a key and pointed to a door on the left. "Through that door and down the hall, last door on your left. There are fresh linens and you can have a pint of beer on us at the bar. Just show the barman your key."

Harry nodded and headed for the room. The room was in an ideal location only five feet from the back entrance. He checked the room quickly them exited through the back door. He walked around to the car and got in.

"We have a room in the back. I'm going to pull the car up to the side of the hotel." He said as started the car and pulled up.

A light drizzle had begun to fall and the cold had replaced the warmth of the afternoon.

"Pull your hat low over your eyes, sir." Harry said to Churchill as he opened the door for him. Churchill groaned and staggered for a moment as the blood flowed back into his legs. Harry steadied him and pulled him along to the back door. He tossed George the room key and George went ahead and opened the room.

Churchill settled himself into one of the overstuffed chairs against the wall. Two beds with matching oak nightstands covered the opposite wall. A small toilet stood behind a door on the left. Harry walked over and turned on the lamp on one of the nightstands.

"Those beds look awful comfortable." Churchill said as he looked over to Harry.

"You pick one, sir. I'm going to go out and see if I can find Sean." He said. Then turning to George, " There's a small bar at the front. You get a free pint with the key. I'm sure the Prime Minister would appreciate it if you were to retrieve one for himself too." Harry winked.

"I'll go pick up a couple pints and then me and Mr. Churchill will enjoy ourselves while you're off hunting." George said as he headed out the door.

"It is very important no one discovers you're here, sir." Harry said to Churchill.

"I know Harry." Churchill grunted as he rose from the chair and scuffled over to the bed. "I'll suffer my pint with George, then retire like a good boy." He winked at Harry while waving him out the door.

Harry smiled and slid out the door.

Outside, the cold enveloped Harry as he walked back around the front of the building and out onto a lane called the Promenade. Harry put his hands in his pocket and flapped his arms in a vain attempt to beat of the chill coming from the sea. Several small pubs lined the Promenade opposite the shore and Harry decided to just step in and check each one as proceeded down the lane.

After walking the length of the Promenade to the south and not having much luck, he turned and started to retrace his steps. As he passed the hotel headed north, two men walked towards him. The men appeared to be drunk, singing Irish ditties as they staggered towards him. Harry smiled, remembering he was in the part of Wales that mostly Irish descendents inhabited.

As Harry stepped aside to allow them to pass and in the middle of a somewhat horrible rendition of 'When Irish Eyes are Smiling", the larger of the two men stopped and turned to Harry.

"Greening' lad." He said, then leaned closer as if to see Harry better. Harry could smell the liquor on his breath as he whispered, "The very likeness of Kathleen, you are!"

Surprised, Harry squinted and took a closer look. The man was huge with a full tangled beard and curly gray hair that shot out from under his cap, dressed in a long weather coat covering the overalls of a fisherman.

"Sean! Is that you?" Harry asked in a low voice.

"As ever there was boy, as ever there was!' The man said a little louder and grasped Harry in a bear hug. "We've had a few pints Harry, but I'm as sober as a new born kitten." He whispered in Harry's ear. As he clapped Harry on the back and stepped back he added, "Now let's go find a private spot to talk"

Harry gasped for air as Sean released him and nodded toward the hotel.

"Kevin. This here's my nephew, Harry! The son of my brother's daughter Kathleen." Sean said as he introduced the other man. The man reached around Sean to shake Harry's hand, "Kevin O'Fallon. Pleased to meet you." He said with a grin. He was clean-shaven with a weather beaten face. He was dressed identical to Sean and appeared to be the same age.

Harry led them around to the back and into the room.

The room was filled with cigar smoke from Churchill's incessant smoking. And true to form Churchill was propped up in bed on top of the bed cover, a bottle of ale in one hand and a cigar in the other. George was sitting on the edge of the other bed with a bottle of ale in his hand. Four unopened and two empty bottles lined the night table between the beds.

"Praise be to Jesus!' Sean burst out when he caught sight of Churchill. He spun around and looked at Harry.

"I figured I was here to carry you and some package to the motherland. Is he the package?" He asked incredulously.

"Part of it. Although not originally." Harry answered and then turned to George who stood up when they entered. "This is my friend George, late of the British Army." He said sweeping his arm towards George.

"George, Kevin O' Fallon and Sean O' Hara, my uncle." Harry completed the introductions.

Both men nodded to George. George nodded in return then sat back on the bed.

Sean turned to Churchill then to Harry with a look that was half anger and half questioning. Harry shrugged and swept his arm out in front of him towards Churchill.

"He goes with the package Sean." He said matter-of-factly.

Sean turned back to Churchill.

"Sir, As an Irishman I don't care for the likes of you much, and if be known I had a hand in helping you escape the Nazis, I may never live it down." He said as he eyed Churchill menacingly.

"Your land has suffered not only under the hands of our armies and politicians, Mr. O'Hara, but also under the hands of your own people. Before you blame the ills of Eire on me, sir, I must remind you that together with your remarkable Mr. Michael Collins, I helped set your country on the right path. Michael was a man of vision, Mr. O'Hara. I wish there had been more we could have done but the rise of the Irish Free State is a start." Churchill said gesturing toward Sean with one of his cigars.

Sean's eyes narrowed as he contemplated what Churchill had said. The mention of 'Big Fella' had stirred deep emotions. Both Sean and Kevin had fought along side Collins in the Irish Republican Army during the struggle that lead to the division of the island nation. He knew that Churchill had carried the referendum in Parliament that gave birth to the Irish Free Republic and that Churchill probably deserved his respect. The lifelong hatred of anything British was hard to squelch but for Harry's sake he would temper his ire.

"Harrumph! Fair enough, Mr. Churchill." He grunted as he started to one of the overstuffed chairs to his left.

"Colonel Warden, sir." Churchill interjected.

Sean looked questioningly at Churchill.

"I am traveling under the name Warden. Colonel Warden. I find it less notable in public." Winston said as he slipped the cigar back into his grinning mouth and saluted Sean with his bottle of ale.

Sean shook his head and chuckled. "Colonel Warden it is." He grinned as he gave Churchill a mock salute and sat.

As if on cue, Kevin moved to the foot of George's bed.

"May I?" he asked as he pointed to the end of the bed.

"Be my guest." George said waving his hand. He reached to the night table, grabbed a bottle and offered it to Kevin. Kevin shook his head and smiled as he reached inside his coat and took out a silver flask, opened it and took a swallow. He winked at George and said "Purely medicinal purposes."

George smiled and offered the bottle to Sean.

"I never deny a free drink when offered!" Sean grinned. Harry took the bottle from George and carried it over to Sean.

"Will you be able to move us tonight Sean?" Harry asked as he sat on the other stuffed chair.

Sean took a big drink and nodded as he swallowed.

"We have the boat tied up in the quay. We arrived yesterday before the German 'invasion'. I don't know if you saw it or not, but the krauts have a patrol boat in these waters."

Harry nodded and said 'Yes. We saw it when we came in. I also saw a couple of German sailors up at the hotel on the hill."

Sean leaned forward interested. "How many did you see lad?" He asked Harry.

"Two." Harry replied.

"That leaves a few unaccounted for. If I'm correct those wee boats have a crew of twelve to fourteen men. If they are ashore tonight, then our chances are much better. How are you going to let the Americans know you're ready?"

"I have a frequency and a short coded message to send to them. Do you have a radio?" Harry asked as he suddenly realized he had taken that part into consideration.

"Not the kind you need. But the Germans do." Sean smiled.

"You mean on the boat?" Harry asked skeptically.

"They need a pretty strong transmitter to talk to their people from up here. Why don't we pay them a visit and borrow their radio?" Sean said as he finished the bottle in one long drink and stood. He looked to George.

"You look like a lad who can handle himself. Care to join us?" Sean asked.

George sprang to his feet. "It would be my pleasure!"

"Those guys are going to be armed. We have a couple of Enfields in the boot of the car." Harry said as he stood.

"George here can get them, lad." Sean said holding his hand up in front of Harry and shaking his head. "This mission of yours is pretty important and we can't have you being hurt or worse. Stay here with Mr…ah, colonel Warden. If anything goes wrong you can still try to get the packages out."

Harry started to protest but George clapped his arm around his shoulder and said, "He's right Harry. The important thing is to keep the man there and the packages safe. If something were to happen to you, it would all come to nothing."

Harry's shoulders sagged and he nodded, knowing George was right. He reached into his back pocket and extracted the letter given to him by Hopkins.

"The code phrase and frequency are written on the bottom." He said as he handed the paper to George.

The three men looked anxious but solemn as they left the room. Harry closed the door behind them, turned and walked dejectedly to the bed George had used.

"Have heart, Harry. I've a feeling your uncle and his friends are very capable people. I believe they'll be successful. The Germans won't expect anyone to board their boat in this village." Churchill said as he straightened his bulk in the bed.

"I suspect we'll need to move fast when they return, sir. They'll surely alert the Germans to our presence." Harry said looking up from the bottle he had grabbed.

"They won't know who we are. They'll definitely be alert to something. But surprise is on our side."

Harry nodded again and pulled himself up cross-wise on the bed leaning against the wall.

They sat in silence, Harry sipping from the bottle, Churchill drinking and smoking.

After about ten minutes, Churchill broke the silence.

"You seem well suited for your role as spy and undercover agent, Harry. I've been impressed by your ingenuity and execution. Perhaps you might want to consider a career change."

Harry looked to Churchill and smiled as he shook his head. "I don't think I'm really cut out for this." He said then seeing the puzzled look on Churchill's face, he continued, "I mean, I really don't put much thought into it. I just react to the situation. But times like now, when I have time to think about it, it fascinates and scares me at the same time."

He looked to Churchill to see if he showed any understanding. Churchill nodded and replied, "Most leaders don't consciously analyze their actions as they go about their tasks. They get a feel for the situation based on gut reaction and then go about the business of getting it done. I've known some great men and they all have that quality. I myself have often had to make quick decisions and very often have to ask my dear Clemmie if I did right. You see, I too second guess myself, although I find that going with the gut reaction seldom is wrong."

Harry pursed his lips, looking at Churchill, digesting what he said. He sighed and leaned back, staring at the ceiling.

"I have to do something, sir. Like you, I don't accept the capitulation of our country. I need to be part of something that will lead to the defeat of the Nazis and the freedom of Britain. But how and where?" Harry leaned forward again and looked at Churchill as he asked, "You'll continue the fight won't you sir? "

"I plan to do what I can. The dominions have already indicated by their refusal to accept the terms of the armistice that they intend to fight on. I believe no matter what Germany does, the Americans will declare war in a day or two. That will be the beginning of the end for Hitler."

"I certainly want to believe you are right. It is hard to imagine how we could come to such a state. Seeing that black uniformed German today at Bletchley really opened my eyes. To think of them all over England is terrifying!" Harry said absently as he re-ran the day's events in his mind.

He had felt no fear when the German made his unexpected appearance, just anger. His love for England was not something he had actually considered, but faced with the knowledge it was to be nevermore provoked an angry sadness in him. He realized it was probably fatigue that made him feel so melancholy and tried to shake the feeling off. He looked intently at Churchill. Churchill was staring at the ceiling with his cigar held to his mouth. He appeared to be in heavy thought. He did not visibly display any turmoil over the situation or the fact he was about to divide the kingdom, but Harry had a feeling it weighed heavily on him.

After a period of silence, Churchill rolled his bulldog head towards Harry.

"You know, Harry. There are a few secrets we have not shared with our American friends, but my guess is some may be as important as Ultra." He said as he removed the cigar from his mouth and reached for the bottle of ale.

"As important as Ultra?" Harry asked. He sensed Churchill was about to impart something very important information.

"It probably isn't too late to gather some of this information and get it to our allies. Of course, Ultra takes precedence. But if someone were to take the time to plan it, as you planned this mission, I'm sure we could succeed in denying our foes some very valuable information." Churchill said as he turned to Harry, raising his brow.

Harry sensed where Churchill was going with this conversation.

"This mission has been successful so far because of luck and the assistance of people who were in a position to open some doors - namely Anthony Eden. With the arrival of the Germans, what will be required will be a lot harder to accomplish. The Germans have spies all over the place as we are beginning to see, and whatever secrets we had won't be secret much longer." Harry replied.

"Britain is a small island but it has many nooks and crannies. It will take time for the Germans even with their notorious organizational skills, to find and analyze them all. I believe, as I am attempting to do, many of the men who have been so beneficial to our conduct of war until now, will be seeking escape. Many brilliant scientists and technicians have been working ceaselessly to create defensive and offensive weapons to aid in our struggle. I think you can see how their efforts could be used to the German's advantage, and prove to be devastating to the Americans and French."

Harry didn't know what kind of weapons Churchill could be talking about. Although he was pretty ignorant of technical advances made by his country, he understood that a lot of effort had been expended by the science community in developing counter measures to Germany's new weapons.

"How would you propose to get whatever secrets you are referring to out? The Germans will soon control the borders and the seas around Britain." Harry finally asked.

"We have controlled our own borders and shores and yet the German's have been able to penetrate them. I think the Americans are capable of figuring out a way." Churchill replied.

Harry watched Churchill for a moment then sat back against the wall. He knew what Churchill was asking, but was he good enough to pull it off? Surely Schellenberg would be looking for him by now. The fire at Bletchley would have raised some sort of an alarm. If it was known he had been there then disappeared it made sense he would be the number one suspect. How would he survive as a hunted man? He did have the advantage of knowing a few people, although it had been so long that he no longer knew what their loyalties would be.

He opened his eyes and glanced at Churchill. Churchill was watching him intently with a bemused smile on his face.

Harry propped himself up on his elbows.

"If the Luftwaffe takes over our airfields, it will be almost impossible for the Americans to lend any kind of assistance in getting information out." He said.

Churchill nodded and replied "As I said before, there are ways if one is determined enough." He set the bottle on the table and pulled himself up into a better sitting position.

"I have no authority to ask you to do any more than you already have. I can't make any promises and truthfully your chances would not be great of going undetected. I have no way of knowing how many troops the Germans plan on using to occupy Britain, but I'll bet the majority will be Gestapo and SS men. They know their job and they can be ruthless. If Schellenberg stays in charge, you'll be a wanted man. He is bound to put two and two together soon."

Harry gave half a smile.

"Your reassurances are noted." He said then added, "What do you think the chances of forming some kind of resistance here would be?"

"Depends how the Germans treat us. If they plan to enslave our people as in France, resistance is inevitable. I am also not too proud to admit that if I can rally an exiled government, perhaps I can change some hearts at home."

Harry considered this. If Churchill succeeded in forming an exiled government, there would be a great many who would support him despite what the current government and King had done to him.

As he contemplated, the door suddenly opened and George burst into the room.

"Gentlemen, let's get moving!" He yelled.

Harry was on his feet in an instant while Churchill struggled to get his bulk out of the bed.

"What's the problem? Did you succeed? Where are Sean and Kevin?" Harry fired the questions at George.

"We got onto the boat all right. There was a minor skirmish with the sentries but none of us got hurt. We got your message out and within a couple of minutes received a reply. We are to meet an American cargo vessel in Dublin. She sails in a few hours so we must hurry. Sean and Kevin are readying their boat and we must meet them at the quay in ten minutes." He helped Churchill to his feet and grabbed the bed cover.

"It's raining and a little chilly out there near the shore. This will help keep the wind out." George told Churchill as he wrapped the bedspread around Churchill's shoulders.

As they headed out the back of the hotel, Harry said, "We'll take the car. The packages are too heavy and bulky to carry."

They bundled into the sedan and headed off towards the quay.

As they turned into the boat landing, they could see the lights still burning on the German boat but there was no sign of life. George pointed towards the north end of the landing and Harry nodded as he saw a single lamp burning on what appeared to be a fishing trawler.

Sean appeared out of the dark as they approached the boat. Harry stopped the car and George leapt out to open the boot.

"Let's hurry lads. I'm afraid it won't be long before someone returns to the German boat." Sean said as he opened the back door to help Churchill out of the car.

Harry ran around the back and assisted George in getting the plans and Enigma. Closing the boot, they scampered after Sean and Churchill.

The trawler was old and showed the wear of the sea on her weather beaten hull. She was about forty feet long and had two long outriggers lashed to her sides as well as netting that hung over the stern. Kevin appeared from below to greet them and help George and Harry with their load.

"We'll put it in the fish hold below and get under way." He said and then turning to Sean, "Sean, get the lines."

Sean left Churchill standing in the middle of the deck and set about the task of freeing the trawler from her moorings. Churchill took a large gulp of sea air and sighed. It was cold and the rain was still falling but he loved the sea and even on an old fishing scow, he knew he would enjoy this trip.

Sean rejoined Churchill and asked if he wished to go below where there was a galley and some rum to warm him up.

"If you don't mind, I'd like to soak up the sea air for a bit." Churchill replied.

"Stay close to the wheel house then. If anyone catches a view of us departing, they won't be able to see you in the shadows." Sean said pointing to the wheelhouse where Kevin and Harry were now headed.

The trawler slowly made its way south then headed west toward the Emerald Isle. Sean returned to the deck and gave Churchill an old oil-skin slicker Sean had given him. Churchill grunted his appreciation and wandered to the port rail to watch the sea pass. The rain lessened as they sailed farther west and with it the chill seemed to lessen.

Harry stayed with Kevin until they were far enough from shore that the lights of Barmouth blended together to form one narrow strip. He then went to join Churchill.

Churchill was leaning on the rail staring out to sea with a bemused look.

"How long does Mr. O'Fallon believe it will take to reach the Irish coast?" Churchill asked as Harry joined him at the rail.

"I think perhaps another hour or hour and a half. The weather has cleared some and the sea is smoothing before us." Harry replied.

"I've given it some thought. If you're intent on keeping the flag waving from distant shores, I'd like to do my part. I mean, if there is more I can do by staying here, then here is where I'll stay." Harry said as he turned and propped his elbows behind him onto the rail.

Churchill reached into his breast pocket and removed a cigar. As he completed the ritual of preparing it, he eyed Harry closely. Harry was staring off to the sea on the far side of the boat. He had a very determined but sad look on his face. The last few days had seemed to harden him, Churchill thought. It was difficult to explain how or why men chose the paths they chose. Having chosen though, few men met destiny with a determination to succeed. Most seemed to tackle life's challenges as if testing their choices to see if perhaps another choice may be best. Harry had made up his mind to complete the task of defeating the forces that had combined to destroy his homeland and Churchill knew Harry would succeed or die trying. He also knew there were other men like Harry who were willing to sacrifice themselves for the same goal. It was because of these men, Churchill knew, he had to continue the fight himself. He had had misgivings of going against his King, but Harry had shown he was right in doing what he must do.

Churchill had succeeded in lighting his cigar despite the wind blowing from the sea. He inhaled a deep drag on the cigar watching as the tip glowed to a bright red, and then removing the cigar, exhaled a long sigh.

"Harry, you've helped me decide that the course of action I seek is right." Churchill finally said. "You are a wonderfully intelligent and talented man. We shall need many more like you in order to ensure our success. However I do not know of any resources I could offer to help you."

"Speak to Mr. Roosevelt. Tell him I'd like to enlist in his intelligence services. Make him understand the importance." Harry said turning to Churchill.

Churchill raised his eyebrows, eyeing Harry for a moment. Shortly, he lowered his gaze and said, "Perhaps you're right. The Americans will have to bear the burden of this war until we can organize again. I don't advocate any British Subject joining another country's armed services, Lord knows we need men ourselves, but in your case, they'll be the only ones with the resources to support you."

Harry saw the sorrow in Churchill's expression and quickly replied, "Make sure you tell him I will not renounce my citizenship. I'll serve the Americans but only as a British Subject."

Churchill brightened as he clapped Harry on the back. "I'll let him know lad. I'm sure he'll agree."

The two turned and watched the sea and the Welsh coast fade behind them in a comfortable silence.

An hour passed as Harry and Churchill broke their silence sporadically with mundane conversation. It served well to keep their thoughts off of the journey they had begun but a few hours ago. Their reverie was broken as George approached.

"We are approaching the Irish coast near Wicklow. Kevin is going to hug the coast north to Dublin. We should be near Dublin in about a half hour."

Harry nodded and reached over to take Churchill by the arm. "Let's go below and get a bit to eat. I don't know when the opportunity will arise again." He said as he led Churchill and George towards the small cabin.

The rain had stopped and a near full moon hung low to the west, silhouetting the hills of the Irish coast. The lights of a train crawled by on the shore headed south as they sailed north. The lights of small villages glowed at intervals along their path. Kevin checked his compass and surveyed the shoreline. He estimated they would begin to see the lights of Dublin very soon. He turned to Sean and nodded. Sean left the wheelhouse and joined the three passengers below.

"We'll soon be entering the waters off Dublin. We'll search for the American vessel and signal them when we enter the harbor. Let's gather your packages and ready yourselves." George said as he entered.

George rose from his chair and followed Sean to the hold. Harry grasped Churchill's shoulder and squeezed a silent goodbye as he followed.

Kevin aimed towards the lighted harbor and began the searched for the American vessel. The harbor was crowded with ships of all nationalities. The neutrals had abandoned England and sailed to Ireland upon the news of the German arrival. He wondered how many Englishmen had sailed with them. It didn't take long to spot the American flag painted on the stern of the big cargo ship. Kevin steered nearer and flashed his fog lamp in Morse towards the wheelhouse of the larger ship. After a few tries, the large ship finally signaled acknowledgement and told Kevin a tug would be sent to meet them. Kevin pulled the throttles to stop and allowed the trawler to drift in the calm waters of the harbor. He turned and watched the men as they brought the packages up to the deck and covered them with a tarp.

On the deck of the trawler, Harry took Sean aside.

"I need to go back Sean. This mission is complete but there is more I need to do." Harry said to.

Astonished, Sean replied, "Go back? Are you daft lad? The Germans will surely be looking for you!"

"I realize that, but there are things that need to get done; things that can't get done if I don't go back. You should understand, Sean. You've been involved in the Troubles for much the same reasons I have now." Harry beseeched Sean.

"Aye lad, perhaps I do understand." Sean said as he clasped Harry's shoulder. "Surely Kathleen will never forgive me lad." He winked.

Harry grinned and said, "Just tell her I was too stubborn. She'll understand that."

Sean nodded and the two men returned to where the others waited.

Harry leaned over to George and told him of his decision.

"Your daft! Harry, that will be suicide!' George cried.

"It may be but I don't intend to die until I'm ready. You know my reasons and I won't change them. You're free to go Sergeant." He smiled at George.

George didn't return the smile. In fact he looked angry.

"I intend to go. I'm no fool! You should re-think this Harry. There are other ways you can fight without entering the enemy's camp." George admonished.

"It's my decision, George. Make sure the old man makes it safely to America. He carries a heavy responsibility." Harry said nodding to Churchill.

"I'll keep an eye on him but I'll accept no responsibility for him. He has a mind of his own, he does. A man would be a fool to accept responsibility for him!" George muttered.

The tug arrived and two American naval officers boarded the tug. Harry shook hands with the officers while George, Sean and Kevin began handing the packages over to the sailors on the tug.

"Captain Lewis sir, and this is Lieutenant Commander Hanlon. The older of the two officers said as he shook Harry's hand.

"Harry Lloyd. You fellows have been briefed on my mission?" Harry asked.

"Not the details, just that we are to collect you and your men along with a package and then hightail it back to New York." Lewis responded as he looked around the trawler. His eyes suddenly widened when he realized who the man in the oil slicker was. He turned to Harry questioningly.

"Colonel Warden?" Harry called Churchill over.

Churchill approached the two officers and extended his hand.

"Colonel Warden, gentlemen." He ginned as he removed the cigar with his free hand.

Mouths agape, both officers shook his hand. Lewis again turned to Harry questioningly.

Harry just looked impassive and said nothing.

"Packages have been loaded." George said to Harry as he joined them.

Harry nodded and said to Lewis, "I guess that concludes my mission. Take care of your charges, Captain."

A still stunned Lewis saluted and replied, "Yes sir!" Turning and taking Churchill by the arm he asked "Colonel?"

Churchill turned and offered his hand to Harry. "You take care lad. I'll make sure the Americans are aware of your importance." He said, then added," Tube Alloys, Harry. That's where the money lies. Tube Alloys."

Harry furrowed his brow and asked, "Tube Alloys sir?"

"Look into it when you get back on the mainland." Churchill winked and turned to follow the Americans back to the tug.

Harry wanted to stop him and ask just what the hell he meant, but thought better of it. Instead he turned to George.

"Better hurry. They need to get underway." He said.

"Ah, hell Harry. I can't leave you to the clutches of the likes of Schellenberg. You'll need someone to watch your back!" He said then waved to the tug. "Off with you lads. I'll be staying." He yelled.

Harry went to protest but as he gathered his argument he heard the horn blast from the tug and saw it begin to pull away. Kevin was already headed to the wheelhouse and Sean stood near the rail watching the tug recede into the waters of the harbor.

'You're a fool George!" Harry said sternly. Underneath, he stifled a smile. Having George watching his back was not a bad thought.

Printed in the United States
6768

9 780595 178551